Confessions of a
Recovering Environmentalist

PAUL KINGSNORTH

CONFESSIONS OF A RECOVERING ENVIRONMENTALIST AND OTHER ESSAYS

Graywolf Press

First published in 2017 by Faber & Faber Limited, London

Extract from 'The Future' by Leonard Cohen © Penguin Random House Canada.

Extract from 'Going, Going', *The Complete Poems of Philip Larkin* by Philip Larkin, edited by Archie Burnett. Copyright © 2012 by The Estate of Philip Larkin. Reprinted by permission of Farrar, Straus and Giroux.

'The Tower Beyond Tragedy', 'Carmel Point', 'Rearmament' and 'The Answer' from *The Collected Poetry of Robinson Jeffers* courtesy of Jeffers Literary Properties.

Extract from 'One Life', *Collected Later Poems, 1988–2000* by R. S. Thomas © Bloodaxe Books, 2004; Extract from 'Other' by R. S. Thomas © The Orion Publishing Group Ltd.

Every effort has been made to trace or contact all copyright holders. The publishers would be pleased to rectify at the earliest opportunity any omissions or errors brought to their notice.

This publication is made possible, in part, by the voters of Minnesota through a Minnesota State Arts Board Operating Support grant, thanks to a legislative appropriation from the arts and cultural heritage fund, and a grant from the Wells Fargo Foundation. Significant support has also been provided by the Lannan Foundation, Target, the McKnight Foundation, the Amazon Literary Partnership, and other generous contributions from foundations, corporations, and individuals. To these organizations and individuals we offer our heartfelt thanks.

Published by Graywolf Press
212 Third Avenue North, Suite 485
Minneapolis, Minnesota 55401

www.graywolfpress.org

Published in the United States of America

ISBN 978-1-55597-780-1

6 8 10 12 11 9 7 5

Library of Congress Control Number: 2016951416

Cover design: Kapo Ng

Cover photograph: Kaidash / Shutterstock

In memory of
Doug Tompkins (1943–2015)

'You've got to get your ass in gear
and do something!'

To function effectively in an environment that precludes everything vital and human is the key to modern life.
  David Foster Wallace

You can best serve civilisation by being against what usually passes for it.
  Wendell Berry

Contents

Epilogue

Introduction: Finding the River

It is hard to see the lion that has eaten you.

Carl Jung

I've heard it said, though I can't remember where, that all writers spend their lives telling the same story, over and over, in different forms, sometimes without even knowing it. When I look back over these essays, I can appreciate the notion. Standing back and observing my own tics and obsessions from a distance, I can see themes emerging like springs from a mountainside. I didn't always recognise them when I wrote them down, but now I can see a river flowing, and I think I can see its direction of travel.

I wrote the first essay in this book in 2009, shortly after the world had ended. Worlds are always ending – that, it turns out, is one of my themes, or tics, or obsessions – and 2008's crisis of capitalism was just the most recent example. In retrospect, the global economic shock of that year looks more like the beginning of some great readjustment rather than a glitch in the machine. It looks less like a failure of markets than a sign of a much deeper malaise, which the previous years of short-term plenty (for some, at least) had disguised or made it easy to put off until another day. The burgeoning human population, a growing food and water crisis, the capture of government by corporate interests, the growing gap between the elites and the rest: everything was meshing into one. And undergirding all of this, and more important than any of it, was the ongoing attack by the industrial wing of humanity on the life of the Earth itself.

I'm writing this introduction two days after a new study about the accelerating decline of Antarctic ice was published in the journal *Nature*. It seems that the decline is faster than was expected, and that its impact will probably be greater than feared. We may now see a sea level rise of up to 5 or 6 feet within the next 85 years; a rate of change that was previously expected to take centuries or even millennia. This, if you'll pardon the dark pun, is only the tip of an ecological iceberg. Extinction levels are higher than they have been for 65 million years. The Earth's atmosphere has not contained as much carbon dioxide as it does today since humanity first evolved. We have eroded half of the Earth's topsoil in just a century and a half, and the rest may last us only another sixty years, as we struggle to feed a ballooning and increasingly demanding human population with less fertile land. I could go on, but I suspect you've heard it all before and that, like the rest of us, you have no idea what to do about it, or whether anything can be done at all.

Worlds are always ending; empires are always falling; the climate has changed before; change is the only constant. These are the comforting stories we tell to get ourselves through the night. These are the words that allow us to continue to avoid looking at the enormity of what we have done and are doing. They allow us to continue to pretend, for a little while longer, that the way we are living is right and normal and inevitable and that it will continue; that these are problems that can be ironed out through the judicious

2

application of our celebrated human cleverness. Does anybody really believe this, down at the cellular level, down in their gut? Sometimes I think that we all know, inside, in the place where we are still wild animals, what we have done. Worlds are always ending, it's true; but not like this. This is new. This is bigger than anything there has ever been for as long as humans have existed, and we have done it, and now we are going to have to live through it, if we can.

By the time I began writing these essays, none of which I expected to end up in a book, this was the conclusion I had come to. Over the years, I had felt fury, frustration, depression, anger, determination and many other, more mixed, emotions as I contemplated the wreck we were making of a bountiful and living world. For most of my twenties, I had put a lot of my energy into environmental activism, because I thought that activism could save, or at least change, the world. By 2008 I had stopped believing this. Now I felt that resistance was futile, at least on the grand, global scale on which I'd always assumed it had to occur. I knew what was already up in the atmosphere and in the oceans, working its way through the mysterious connections of the living Earth, beginning to change everything. I saw that the momentum of the human machine – all its cogs and wheels, its production and consumption, the way it turned nature into money and called the process growth – was not going to be turned around now. Most people didn't want it to be; they were enjoying it. All the arguments, all the colourful campaigns, all the well-researched case studies were just washing up on the beach and expiring quietly on the sand, like exhausted jellyfish. There was no stopping what we had unleashed. We were going to eat everything, including ourselves. It was locked in now. It was too late.

My incentive for putting pen to paper at this point was simple: I was trying to work out what I thought about all this, and what to do next, and how to stay sane as I did so. Much of the resulting prose was first published either in the books or on the website of the Dark Mountain Project, which I founded in that same year, 2009. Inspired by the Modernist manifestos that had appeared a century before, at another time of global upheaval, I had drafted, with a fellow writer, Dougald Hine, a little manifesto called *Uncivilisation*, which was intended to act as a challenge to artists and writers. The manifesto declared (manifestos always declare; they're noisy things) that we were not facing a crisis of economics or politics or technology, but a crisis of stories – that the tales we were telling ourselves about our place in the world were dangerously wrong, that we needed to right them and that this was at least in part a job for writers, artists and anyone else who played with the imagination for some semblance of a living. I suppose now that this was a challenge to myself as much as to anyone else: could we do better? Could I?

I have a quote pinned up above my writing desk. It's dirty and stained, because it has been there for years. It's from George Orwell's essay on Henry Miller, *Inside the Whale*. Orwell, writing about Miller's fiction, makes a typically stark claim. 'Good novels', he declares, 'are not written by ortho-doxy-sniffers, nor by people who are conscience-stricken about their own unorthodoxy. Good novels are written by people who are *not frightened*.' Orwell, I think, must also have been challenging himself when he wrote those words. It was a good challenge; I've tried to adopt it myself, and not just for my fiction. I have tried, in these essays, not to be frightened by the consequences of where my attempts at thinking were leading me. I have tried not to lie to myself about the state of the world; not to tell myself, or anyone else, what we all wanted to hear. I haven't always succeeded; maybe I haven't succeeded at all. I'm sure I could have been braver. But I have done my best to try to be clear-headed and clear-eyed.

Most of the essays in this book were originally published between 2010 and 2016, in an eclectic variety of publications. Most appear here in the form in which they were first published, though a few have been edited very slightly to avoid repetition and to repair any retrospective factual holes. One of the essays, 'Learning What to Make of It', is published for the first time here.

Looking back, trying to find the river, I see now that the story winding itself through this book is the breaking of the link between people and places, between the past and the present, between instinct and reason, and all the consequences that have ensued and will ensue. I see that it is the silencing of what Thomas Berry called 'the great conversation' between humans and the rest of nature, and what this means. This book is about feeling lost, and trying to find a way again in a world remaking itself at incredible speed, a world racing away from the real towards artifice and a narrow human narcissism. Our direction of travel is clear, but our destination is not. The old is dead or dying, but the new has yet to be born. At times like these, I'm not sure anybody really has any useful answers. But maybe it is possible to at least pin down some useful questions. I have tried to do that here.

County Galway, Ireland, April 2016

I : COLLAPSE

A Crisis of Bigness

Living through a collapse is a curious experience. Perhaps the most curious part is that nobody wants to admit it's a collapse. The results of half a century of debt-fuelled 'growth' are becoming impossible to deny convincingly, but even as economies and certainties crumble, our appointed leaders bravely hold the line. No one wants to be the first to say the dam is cracked beyond repair.

To listen to a political leader at this moment in history is like sitting through a sermon by a priest who has lost his faith but is desperately trying not to admit it, even to himself. Watch your chosen president or prime minister mouthing tough-guy platitudes to the party faithful. Listen to them insisting in studied prose that all will be well. Study the expressions on their faces as they talk about 'growth' as if it were a heathen god to be appeased by tipping another cauldron's worth of fictional money into the mouth of a volcano.

In times like these, people look elsewhere for answers. A time of crisis is also a time of opening up, when thinking that was consigned to the fringes moves to centre stage. When things fall apart, the appetite for new ways of seeing is palpable, and there are always plenty of people willing to feed it by coming forward with their pet big ideas.

But here's a thought: what if big ideas are part of the problem? What if, in fact, the problem is bigness itself?

The crisis currently playing out on the world stage is a crisis of growth. Not, as we are regularly told, a crisis caused by too little growth, but by too much of it. Banks grew so big that their collapse would have brought down the entire global economy. To prevent this, they were bailed out with huge tranches of public money, which in turn is precipitating social crises on the streets of Western nations. The European Union has grown so big, and so unaccountable, that it threatens to collapse in on itself. Corporations have grown so big that they are overwhelming democracies and building a global plutocracy to serve their own interests. The human economy as a whole has grown so big that it has been able to change the atmospheric composition of the planet and precipitate a mass-extinction event.

One man who would not have been surprised by this crisis of bigness, had he lived to see it, was Leopold Kohr. Kohr has a good claim to be the most interesting political thinker that you have never heard of. Unlike Karl Marx, he did not found a global movement or inspire revolutions. Unlike Friedrich Hayek, he did not rewrite the economic rules of the modern world. Kohr was a modest, self-deprecating man, but this was not the reason his ideas have been ignored by movers and shakers in the half-century since they were produced. They have been ignored because they do not flatter the egos of the power-hungry, be they revolutionaries or plutocrats. In fact, Kohr's message is a direct challenge to them. 'Wherever something is wrong,' he insisted, 'something is too big.'

Kohr was born in 1909 in the small Austrian town of Oberndorf. This small-town childhood, together with his critical study of economics and political theory at the London

School of Economics, his experience of anarchist city states during the Spanish Civil War, which he covered as a war reporter, and the fact that he fled Austria after the Nazi invasion contributed to his growing suspicion of power and its abuses. Settling in the United States, Kohr began to write the book that would define his thinking. Published in 1957, *The Breakdown of Nations* laid out what at the time was a radical case: that small states, small nations and small economies are more peaceful, more prosperous and more creative than great powers or superstates. It was a claim that was as unfashionable as it was possible to make. This was the dawn of the space age – a time of high confidence in the progressive, gigantist, technology-fuelled destiny of humankind. Feted political thinkers were talking in all seriousness of creating a world government as the next step towards uniting humanity. Kohr was seriously at odds with the prevailing mood. He later commented, drily, that his critics 'dismissed my ideas by referring to me as a poet'.

Kohr's claim was that society's problems were not caused by particular forms of social or economic organisation, but by their size. Socialism, capitalism, democracy, monarchy – all could work well on what he called 'the human scale': a scale at which people could play a part in the systems that governed their lives. But once scaled up to the level of modern states, all systems became oppressors. Changing the system, or the ideology that it claimed inspiration from, would not prevent that oppression – as any number of revolutions have shown – because 'the problem is not the thing that is big, but bigness itself'.

Drawing from history, Kohr demonstrated that when people have too much power, under any system or none, they abuse it. The task, therefore, was to limit the amount of power that any individual, organisation or government could get its hands on. The solution to the world's problems was not more unity but more division. The world should be broken up into small states, roughly equivalent in size and power, which would be able to limit the growth and thus domination of any one unit. Small states and small economies were more flexible, more able to weather economic storms, less capable of waging serious wars, and more accountable to their people. Not only that, but they were more creative. On a whistle-stop tour of medieval and early modern Europe, *The Breakdown of Nations* does an entertaining job of persuading the reader that many of the glories of Western culture, from cathedrals to great art to scientific innovations, were the product of small states.

To understand the sparky, prophetic power of Kohr's vision, you need to read *The Breakdown of Nations*. Some of it will create shivers of recognition. Bigness, predicted Kohr, could lead only to more bigness, for 'whatever outgrows certain limits begins to suffer from the irrepressible problem of unmanageable proportions'. Beyond those limits it was forced to accumulate more power in order to manage the power it already had. Growth would become cancerous and unstoppable, until there was only one possible endpoint: collapse.

We have now reached the point that Kohr warned about over half a century ago: the point where 'instead of growth serving life, life must now serve growth, perverting the very purpose of existence'. Kohr's 'crisis of bigness' is upon us and, true to form, we are scrabbling to tackle it with more of the same: closer fiscal unions, tighter global governance, geoengineering schemes, more economic growth. Big, it seems, is as beautiful as ever to those who have the unenviable task of keeping the growth machine going.

This shouldn't surprise us. It didn't surprise Kohr, who, unlike some of his utopian critics, never confused a desire for radical change with the likelihood of it actually happening. Instead, his downbeat but refreshingly honest conclusion was that, like a dying star, the gigantist global system would in the end fall in on itself, and the whole cycle of growth would begin all over again. But before it did so, 'between the intellectual ice ages of great-power domination', the world would become 'little and free once more'.

Guardian, 2011

Upon the Mathematics of the Falling Away

'If you think I am wandering here, hold your tits or your balls or hold somebody else's. Everything fits here.'

I: CONTROL

'What matters most is how you walk through the fire.'

Four years ago, someone very close to me committed suicide. I don't talk about this much, and I still don't know what I feel about it.

This is not a short story.

This is non-fiction.

I know this makes it harder for you, and I'm sorry about that.

When I got the phone call I was picking camomile flowers in my back garden. That sounds twee and bucolic, but it was a tiny, urban back garden and the flowers were there when we moved in and I didn't want to waste them. I quite like camomile tea. I don't know why I'm explaining myself.

One of the thoughts I had not long after hearing the news was how I could eventually write about this; the thing itself, and all the horrors that had led up to the thing. I knew that one day I was going to have to. I then felt guilty about thinking this, not because I thought it was the wrong thing to be thinking but because I knew I ought to think that it

was the wrong thing to be thinking. It was selfish and cal-
culating and slightly psychopathic, and these are all things
that nobody ought to be at any time, let alone at a time like
this. What could I do? It was just what came into my head.

This is not a short story. I'm sorry.

When your world collapses you tell yourself that you
couldn't see it coming, but you could see it coming. You
wait for it to 'sink in' but it never 'sinks in' because you are
not made of quicksand, you are made of glass. It never sinks
in at all, it just glances off and then comes a glimmer of light
as the sun goes down and then you just feel guilty for ever.

Other people tell you things too. Mostly they tell you
that it's not your fault, and them telling you this makes no
difference to anything. You know, not so far down, not so
well hidden, that it is your fault, will always be your fault,
you know this as well as you know anything that is true or
is not true. But everyone tells you it anyway because they
are trying to be kind and they don't know what they're talking about.

I will tell you the secret thing about suicide. The secret
thing about suicide is that it is enticing. People who have
lived through the suicides of others or who have seen the
consequences or suffered them do not like to hear people
say this. Suicide is not glamorous, they say. This is true.
Dead bodies are not glamorous. Baths full of two-day-old
blood are not glamorous. Every glass of red wine you drink
for months afterwards; it never leaves. But suicide is still
enticing. It is enticing because suicide is protest, suicide is
wilful disobedience. It pisses in the face of progress and all
its wan little children, sucking so desperately at the with-
ered teat of immortality. Suicide is good because suicide is

one hard, sharp scream at the meaning of what we pretend to think we are. Chatterton, Plath, Curtis, Cobain: pick a card. Trade it in if the meaning is not quite to your liking. Somebody will speak to you in the end.

Suicide is everywhere in this culture, under every stone, and once you come to be a part of that great, unspeaking clan of people who have been touched by it, you see this. Three years ago, my wife and I had a baby daughter. Before she was born I never noticed babies except when they annoyed me in cafes. Now I see babies everywhere. The streets are full of toddlers; they cascade from the doorways and overflow from the drains. Experience changes you. Nothing else changes you.

Birth is worshipped; death is feared; suicide is held under. We are the Men of the West.

Suicide has often enticed me. Not in the sense that I have thought about doing it to myself, not really, not often. Only in the sense that a forbidden thing will attract damaged and curious souls more surely than anything else. Why would somebody do this? What would they hope to gain? Why would they not leave a note? Not even a note.

Suicide is everywhere and nowhere. We are coming to it, all of us, in our own time. It circles us like the Wild Hunt, howling for the blood of Men, and we crane our necks to see it pass across the face of the harvest moon. Perhaps it will call to us. Perhaps we will be chosen. Do not choose us. Choose us!

Some suicides are a final, defiant act of control. This was my experience. They say: I control my death, I control how my death is seen, and I control the consequences. I do this. Me. Not you. Me. I decide.

You tell yourself that you couldn't see it coming, but you could see it coming. I know what I'm talking about on this one. It never sinks in.

This is not a short story.

II: ASH

'I'm for the true human spirit, wherever it is, wherever it has been hiding.'

Everybody else in the world has already written about this, but I am going to do it anyway. Something is rising to the surface today.

I was due to fly in to New York on an American Airlines flight from Mexico City on 12 September 2001. I had been in Chiapas for six weeks, living with Zapatistas and learning Spanish and feeling radical and young, and I didn't want to go. But I had never been to the US before, and it is impossible not to want to. Which citizen of a windswept backwater of empire does not want to see Rome?

I got up on the morning of 11 September and took to the streets of Mexico City, hunting for breakfast. I am self-absorbed at the best of times, but when I am hungry I am a black hole.

There was a strange atmosphere, which I mostly ignored.

I found a cafe which opened out into the street. A group of men were gathered around a television fixed high on a wall. A building was burning. Some disaster film. I stopped to watch, but couldn't make out what was going on.

A man turned to me. 'New York,' he said, indicating the TV with a nod of his head.

'Oh, right,' I replied, non-committally. What was he telling me that for? I went looking for the menu.

It was days before I got it. When the airline told me that afternoon that my flight was cancelled and they didn't know when there would be another, I thought only of myself. No flights! To New York! What was this, World War Three? What a lot of shitting about for nothing. What an overreaction.

Possibly it was World War Three, it just didn't feel like it at the time.

When I got to America, I quickly realised that I'd been there before. I spent a month or so in the States, and I felt like that all the time. New York was *Annie Hall* and *Ghostbusters*. The Nevada Desert was *Close Encounters*. San Francisco was *Easy Rider* and *Tales of the City* and *Escape from Alcatraz*. The Utah Flats were *High Plains Drifter*. LA was hell. I drove along Route 66 (*Badlands*) and stayed in motels (*Psycho*) and ate pastrami (*The Godfather*) and all of it was dulled by knowing what came in the next reel. Steam really did come out of vents in the New York streets (*Taxi Driver*). I felt like I'd come home, which excited me and made me feel lost and worried.

Twenty-First Century Syndrome: knowing a place so well that you're bored by the time you first visit.

What I remember most about New York was the ash. There was ash everywhere, literally everywhere. On the streets, on the tops of mailboxes, on cars, on rooftops. I walked down every street running my fingers through the thick, grey ash that had gathered on the sills of the windows. It glinted like iron pyrites; there was something in it that glinted.

The closer you got to where the World Trade Center had been, the thicker the ash got. I went there and gawped like a ghoul through the steel-mesh fences, pretending to stand in silent solidarity, hoping to see bodies. The hellish heap of rubble was still on fire. The ash was in the air. The city stank, and was very quiet.

Near the mount of burning stone, in every doorway near to that place and leaning up against lamp posts and tied to windows and in the windshields of cabs and cars were hastily erected boards, hand-drawn posters, notes. On each was written the name of somebody missing. Often there were photos. Have you seen my son? His name is Oscar. He may have lost his memory. He may be injured. Please phone. Please phone.

The ash I had seen before, and the tsunami of fire that had canyoned between the tall buildings, and the collapsing skyscrapers. *Independence Day. King Kong.* But these agonised denials of reality, these horrible screams into the void, this pain and fear and loneliness, the scrawls and the smiles and the dissolving hope that came with them: this was new. This was original. No scriptwriter had thought of this one, not in any film that I'd seen.

III: CHESS

'Strange thoughts are much like hangovers: you feel better without them.'

I had never seen anything like Jakarta before. The finely balanced chaos of a great city in what we have now learned to call the 'developing world' (They are well on their way to

19

becoming Us; there is no need to panic) is something impossible to understand unless you have seen it. It is an untuned instrument that somehow plays a cohesive melody. Who is in charge here? No one is in charge here. This machine runs on its own energy, its own internal logic. This is anarchy in action. The first time you see anarchy in action you are wary, scared, and then later you are thrilled and then you want to throw it all away and join the circus. But you never can because you do not belong here and you never will, and in any case when you face with honesty the dirt and the squalor of this you want, actually, to fly home and take a bath and feel relieved and then begin to arrange your colourful photos in chronological order.

I was twenty-one. It was the first time I had seen the poverty and desperation and colour and creative electricity of the great slum cities of the poor world. I was a tourist. There was a group of us, and we were staying in a hotel down some grubby backpacker alley, which to me seemed impossibly exotic. If I had brought a linen suit I could have pretended to be Graham Greene, but I didn't know what linen suits were when I was twenty-one, and I'd not read any Graham Greene either. I didn't know much when I was twenty-one, which was why I thought I knew everything.

I can't remember the guy's name, but he was in our party and he was one of those posers I took an instant dislike to. He might have had dreadlocks. He certainly wore combat trousers and, despite being about the same age as me, was working hard to exhibit a man-of-the-world insouciance that stirred envy and irritation in me at the same time. This Jeremy had already spent a few months trawling around Asia with various Tabithas and Quentins and was full of stories, most of them probably lies, about his daring adventures.

On our first night in the exotically hot and dirty hostel, this guy disappeared for an hour or so, out onto the street. I thought he was stupid and naive, was probably being knifed or robbed or angrily stripped by a baying mob, and I was feeling smug and teachery about this when he turned up again. It seemed that Jeremy had made friends with a couple of locals in the street and had been playing chess with them. Chess! In Jakarta! On the street! With locals! Christ.

What was wrong with this? Everything was wrong with this. I didn't know why; it just seemed wrong that Jeremy should be so confident, so big, while I was so small. Making friends with Indonesians in the street! Playing chess with them! I didn't even know how to play chess. I wouldn't have known how to speak to an Indonesian. Fuck Jeremy. Why wasn't I more like him?

Jakarta was great back then because Jakarta was a tyranny, and tyrannies are great for tourists. These were the Suharto years, the dog days of the waning dictator's grip over this great, sprawling country. The general, who had seized power in a coup thirty years before, had liquidated so many communists, tribespeople, opponents, rivals and even family members that his hold on power, for now, seemed assured. His face looked down from the wall of every rural police station and city school. He had his spies everywhere, they said.

The chaos I had seen was chaos because it was permitted to be chaos. You could play chess with locals in the street under Suharto because Suharto, unseen, up there, was holding this all together. These 17,000 islands, these 700 languages, these 300 ethnicities, this great bright, impossible archipelago empire: it hung together, it avoided chaos, collapse, disintegration, because of the strong hand, because of the weapons my government was selling the strong hand.

A few years later the dictator fell, brought down by feckless markets and hungry people. That was when the falling away began for Indonesia; the breaking apart, the dissolving. It is still going on over there, still working its way out, like the moves in a chess game. Before the chaos, the calm that is moulded by the will of the strong seems as if it is simply The Way Things Are. But the strong are not what they used to be.

I've learned, since then, how to play chess. I play it very badly. When I play chess I can think I am in the running, I can feel like I have things in hand, I can be planning ahead, feeling a surge of excitement rising within me – It could actually happen this time! I could actually win! – and then, suddenly, from nowhere: bang! Checkmate. How did that happen? Where did that come from? Afterwards, it's as obvious as daylight. But afterwards is too late. Afterwards is no bloody use to anyone.

IV: HOME

'You begin saving the world by saving one person at a time; all else is grandiose romanticism or politics.'

As I get older, my ambition drains away. I like this, although sometimes it worries me too.

When I was in my early twenties I was desperate to be famous and I had no idea why. These days, knowing more about why, the idea increasingly appals me. These days my role model is not Hemingway but Salinger. I will hide from them all. I will be photographed by men in hedges on my way back from doing the shopping. I will be Emily Dickinson. Publishing is for the weak. I will write and write and write and stick the lot, all anyhow, in my desk drawers. They can sort it out when I'm dead. Why would I care? I don't write for them anyway.

I used to long to be on *Newsnight* every week, offering up my Very Important Opinions to the world. This was in my twenties, back when I didn't know anything. Only people who don't know anything want to be noticed for offering up their opinions as if they were facts. I don't know why or when I lost my hunger for this, but now it only occasionally bubbles up to the surface, a pale reminder of what I used to be, like a few strands on the head of a bald man, left to waft in the breeze for old time's sake.

Over time, I did enough of this stuff to realise how little I wanted to do it. I wrote columns for the smart newspapers and the clever magazines, I went onto *PM* and *Today* on Radio 4 to argue about God knows what – I can't even remember, it matters so little. I went on TV a bit too; I even, it pains me to say, sat on the sofa with Richard and Judy. This is absolutely true. Jerry Springer was sitting next to me. It was . . . strange.

I did the big book stuff as well, and before I was thirty. Got paid big advances, got flown across the world to speak at book festivals, got extracts from my books run big across the centre pages of mass-market papers. I shouldn't complain; I don't complain. I just don't want it any more, not like that. I don't want to be on TV, I don't want to be feted,

I don't want to worry about where my book is on the Amazon charts. I have stopped believing that I am important. I feel small. It feels like a great freedom, a true release.

I sometimes worry that I have given up, caved in, lost my spark, but actually it's not my spark I've lost, just my vanity. Most of it, anyway. I wonder, as I write this, whether that suicide four years ago sucked it out of me, and I think now that if that isn't true it ought to be, and not just for reasons of narrative closure.

Look: here's how it is, how it seems to me right now. Life is a series of collapses, staggered and staggering. If there is a trick – and we seem to think there always ought to be – then maybe it is simply to remember that collapse is not always bad. Death is not always bad. Suicide: maybe even suicide is not always bad. Or if it is, if it is always irretrievably bad, at least maybe it is not always your fault. Lose something, let go of it as it falls away, and you may gain something else. Or you may not, but at least if you have let go, said your goodbyes, accepted your given load – then maybe you can watch it fall with lighter shoulders.

These days my desire, overpowering sometimes, is for some land. An acre or two, some bean rows. A pasture, broadleaved trees, a view of a river. A small house, my kids running about. Solidity, hard ground beneath me, something there to stop me sinking. Clean air, food, meat, water. Family, earth, mud, all the small wonders and irritations of life rising up to meet me as I come home. Having a home.

Everything falls away in the end, or sooner. Collapse comes every autumn. Sooner or later your vanity will go, too, and then you will discover where you are in the cycle and that the cycle cannot be halted. Then you will have to

lower your shoulders, not raise them, as the rain gets up.
You will have to attend to your smallness, then.
   Everything falls away in the end. It's not your fault. It's
just the way it is. It's fine.
   It's all going to be fine.

*All quotes are from the varied and various works of the
late Charles Bukowski, who also provided the inspiration
for the title.*

Dark Mountain, issue 2, 2011

The Drowned World

Here in Cumbria, in the far north-west of England, we've been experiencing what are called 'extreme weather events' for nearly a year. Compared to what, say, the Caribbean coast experiences every year, these 'events' are pretty small beer, but for England, a country whose landscape is a lot more modest than its politicians or its football team, they count as extreme.

Last autumn we had the biggest floods in living memory. People were helicoptered out of their houses and entire towns disappeared under eight feet of burst river. Then we had the hardest winter for decades, in which the roads were sheets of ice for weeks and I regularly had to ask the farmer to tow me up the hill with his tractor because my van wouldn't make it. As I write, in July 2010, we are in the middle of the driest summer since 1929.

While this is bad news for my struggling broad beans, it does allow a rare glimpse of a drowned past. The levels of Haweswater, the easternmost lake of the English Lake District in which I live, are currently exceptionally low, and this has brought the ghost village of Mardale Green up into the light for the first time in decades.

The story of Mardale Green has entranced me since I first heard it as a child, when I walked in the valley. Haweswater is today a long, empty stretch of water in a valley whose only outstanding features are spiritless squares of plantation pines. In some lights it's an eerie place; you can sense some kind of loss there, an emptiness that hangs around in the air. There's a reason for this, and it's below the water's surface.

In its natural state, Haweswater was two smaller lakes known as High and Low Water, which were separated by a narrow spit of land. They were fringed by trees and meadows, and their shores were dotted with farmsteads. At the head of the valley stood the village of Mardale Green, with its typical cluster of Westmorland stone houses, a medieval church and an inn, the Dun Bull.

Haweswater's valley is a dead end: there is no way, except on foot, to cross the mountain ridge known as High Street which blocks it at its western end (though the Romans managed to build a road that today still runs along this ridge; it's a giddying achievement, often literally). Haweswater's isolated valley community, its landscape and history, were by no means unique in this region; in many ways it was typical of Lakeland life before the coming of modernity. It was tethered to its place and to its lineage, and many of its people knew nothing else.

I wonder, then, how the villagers felt in 1919 when they heard that the Manchester Water Corporation had secured the passing of the Haweswater Act, enabling the compulsory purchase of the valley, the construction of a dam at its eastern end and the drowning of everything in the vicinity, including Mardale Green. I wonder at the clash of cultures; at how the coming loss was conceived and assimilated by the farming families, the hunters and the shepherds whose water came from the local becks and who had no telephone lines or electricity. The new reservoir was being built to provide drinking water for the burgeoning population of the city of Manchester. For the city to grow, a village, and a way of life, had to die.

It was all a painted miniature: progress in a nutshell. Great armies of labourers were brought in to build the dam as the locals looked on. A new village was built to house the workers and their families, for the Haweswater project would take years. Unlike the existing village, this new, twentieth-century prefab settlement had electricity, pool tables, radios, washing machines – all of the promises that the new age was bringing. Construction of the dam took ten years. During that time, life in Mardale Green went on as it had for centuries, only now with the shadow of its own end hanging over it, lengthening by the day.

The dam's plug was finally set two decades after the project had been given the go-ahead. Most of the village's buildings were blown up by the Royal Engineers before the flood. The Holy Trinity church held an emotional last service for the villagers that was also attended by hundreds of people from outside the valley – so many that most had to listen to Mardale's farewell outside on the grass through speakers rigged up by a local radio ham. The church was then dismantled stone by stone. Bodies were dug up from the churchyard and re-interred in nearby Shap. Some of the stone was used to build the take-off tower for the new reservoir, in which the old church windows can still be seen.

The waters swallowed Mardale Green in 1939, as the world's first fully industrialised war swallowed Western civilisation. Today, in 2010, the old stone walls that surrounded the pastures, and the shells of some of the old buildings, have come up into the light again above the lowered surface of Haweswater. The old fields are bleached white, and the remains of the drystone walls are black and slimy.

What happened to Mardale Green is still happening, on a bigger scale and with more pain attached, across the planet. In China, more than 1.2 million people have been forcibly displaced to make way for the Three Gorges Dam: a dubious world record. In India, the Narmada Bachao Andolan have been fighting for decades to stop the Indian government building a series of over three thousand dams in the Narmada valley, displacing hundreds of thousands of people and destroying pristine ecosystems.

The story is always the same. An expanding economy needs water, or electric power, or both. Dams and reservoirs are planned, in the interests of national development and economic competitiveness. Villagers whose lifestyles are genuinely 'low impact' and 'sustainable' are barged out of the way, often in the most horrific circumstances, by a metastasising urban culture that claims to want to be both of these things but is not willing to pay the hard price. The city eats the country.

The line from the authorities is always the same too: this is for everyone's benefit. The reality is usually different; the power and the piped water go to the industrial areas, the cities, the rich suburbs. The refugees from the country go to the slums. Who notices? Who reports it? A few journalists and campaigners, but most of us never hear of these things, or care if we do.

It wasn't so long ago that big dams had a bad name. Initially hailed as energy saviours in the late nineteenth century, by the late twentieth the huge destruction of ecosystems and cultures that their construction usually required had become too big to ignore. But it was still not as big as the demand for the power and water that dams provide the ever-spreading Machine. Today, mega-dams are as popular as ever, and are often dressed up as yet another 'renewable solution' to the climate change caused by the development model they were originally part of. It's the same old mutton, now dressed up as low-carbon lamb, and we are still hooked on it. It gives us – some of us – power, order, control, national pride. It allows us to grow, for a while. We can drown the past, and much of the inconvenient present, under hundreds of feet of water and hope it never rises again to show us what's beneath the surface.

Strangely, as I have been writing this it's started to rain outside; the first rain in weeks. It's heavy and fresh. What can be seen of Mardale Green will be no doubt be gone again soon, and Manchester will be able to breathe easier. Here in Cumbria we'll be able to use our hosepipes to wash our cars down and water our herbaceous borders without having to worry about it. Everything will go back to normal.

dark-mountain.net, 2010

The Space Race Is Over

It was perhaps most popular in the 1950s, as a new consumer society began confidently rolling off the production line, and the age of literary science-fiction arguably reached its peak. It was particularly popular with children, who read about it in comics with titles like *Fantastic Adventures* and *Planet Stories*. But many adults were equally sold on the promise offered. It was assumed fairly widely that by the year 2000 the promise would have been kept, and that humanity would benefit greatly.

It didn't take long for this optimism to abate, and for a few decades the idea seemed to disappear from the popular consciousness. But I've noticed that in the last few years that old promise has resurfaced in the popular consciousness. This time around, though, it has a different taste to it. This time around, it seems more like a threat.

I'm referring to the human colonisation of other worlds. It seems eccentric even to write the words, but there's no doubt that a belief in humanity's need – perhaps its destiny – to colonise the Moon, or Mars, or other worlds known or unknown, is making a strange kind of cultural comeback. No matter that it is no more practical now than it was in the 1950s. No matter that it doesn't look likely that it could happen within the lifetime of anyone alive today, if ever. The practicalities are not the point: it is a fantasy, a motif. It is a means of salvation.

Back in the optimistic 1950s, with the promise of material abundance everywhere, the space race beginning, and much of the population of the Western world still excited about the possibilities offered by new technologies and a benign, avuncular science, the idea of humans some day extending their reach to other worlds seemed simply an inevitable progression. I remember believing it myself at school in the late 1970s and the early 1980s. This was the future, and it looked great. I consumed Isaac Asimov novels at a rate of knots. I was looking forward to it.

Today, the world is a different place. The popular faith in science and technology has drained away, to be replaced by a widespread, if often unspoken, fear. From biotechnology to geoengineering, from Reaper drones to internet surveillance, the democratic promise of technology has been transmuted into an authoritarian threat. Meanwhile, that vision of science-fuelled progress has done as much damage as it has offered improvement. With the climate changing, with the sixth mass extinction well under way, with the ocean swimming in our industrial refuse, with our own chemical backwash in our breast milk and bloodstreams, it's a harder world for techno-optimists to find a voice. We have opened the box and seen where our ambition leads, and though we might quickly close it again and look away, it is too late in the day for any kind of innocence.

I think it is precisely this fear of the future, this feeling that we have unleashed a monster that is now beyond our control, that has given rise to the latest cultural outburst about the colonisation of other worlds. This time, the idea is not buoyed on a tide of optimism and hope, but tinged with desperation, sadness and sometimes even anger. This time, it is not our next exciting adventure, but our final hope.

Just in the last few years, I have seen a number of people who should know better speculating about how colonising Mars may be humanity's best prospect for a liveable future. The logic verges on the psychopathic: we have now wrecked this planet beyond the point of no return; there are too many people here, our political systems are unable to contain our technological or economic ambitions, and individual greed and desire is running out of control. There is no way that 9 billion people can live the kind of lifestyle they apparently want to live without endless conflict and ecological destruction.

The solution? Not to change ourselves, but to find another planet on which to replay the same script. If we begin to shift people 'offworld', we will have new frontiers to explore. The pressure on Earth will be reduced. We will be saved, by our cleverness, from the consequences of our cleverness.

Some of the voices that have been clamouring for humans to build themselves a presence on other worlds have been predictable enough. Astronaut Buzz Aldrin, for example, a veteran of those optimistic times, called last year for 'American permanence on the planet Mars' within two decades. Stephen Hawking, probably the world's most famous pop-scientist, recently insisted that 'We must continue to go into space for humanity . . . We won't survive another thousand years without escaping our fragile planet.'

Physicists and astronauts can be excused their daydreams, but they are no longer alone. New strands have been woven into the optimistic space rhetoric of earlier times, and one of the most common is the suggestion that colonising other worlds will provide new space for humans to expand –

and, perhaps crucially, may offer new resources for the toys, gadgets and machines we are mining our own planet to death to get hold of. Writing in the millionaire's magazine of choice *Forbes* last year, technology writer James Conca made this case starkly: 'Growing shortages of key inorganic elements, such as rare earth elements for all our electronic gadgets and renewable energy systems, platinum and other related metals . . . suggest that we may need more non-renewable resources than Earth can provide.'

You will find arguments like this in every niche on the internet now: we need more space, we need more stuff, and we can't find it here. Maybe it is 'out there' instead! Bind this bundle of blind greed and desire with a length of imperial bombast – insist that exploring space is the equivalent of exploring the oceans in an earlier age, that it is our right and our destiny – and you have a whole new fantastical mythology on your hands. Now, the planet that created us is what holds us back from achieving our potential. Note how Hawking talks of 'escaping' the Earth, as if the only living planet we know of, the source of all life, were a prison, and the dead vacuum of space offered the clean air of freedom. It takes a strange kind of mind to believe this. Perhaps it takes a brilliant one. 'There are some ideas so absurd', wrote George Orwell, 'that only an intellectual could believe them.'

At the same time as this seed has begun to re-establish itself in the intellectual topsoil of the industrial world, I have seen other utopian weeds begin to flourish. I recently had a conversation with a woman who told me she was looking forward to the development of the artificial uterus – a technology that is currently being explored – so that women could be relieved of the burden of pregnancy and birth. She believed it would foster gender equality.

Perhaps related to this is the ever popular dream of the 'Singularity' – itself a term coined in the 1950s. The Singularity is the point at which machine intelligence surpasses human intelligence, and all bets are off about the future of our species (and presumably every other species too). The Singularity is an idea that used to be confined to the hipster idealists of Silicon Valley, but it has recently broken free and is beginning to establish itself more widely.

There is plenty more technological utopianism that could be added to this list: the ongoing crusade by neo-environmentalists to use biotechnology to recreate extinct species, for example. Or perhaps even the increasingly dominant concept of the 'Anthropocene' era, the Age of Humans, in which we have changed the Earth so radically that our only option is to act as if we were not simply inhabitants but creators: to take on the mantle of gods in order to correct our mistakes. For a culture that pivots around a need for control and a deeply anthropocentric idea of human manifest destiny, the appeal of this notion is clear enough.

What are we to make of this? Is it some strange, deranged endgame? Perhaps techno-industrial society, hyped up on its own sense of indestructibility, is hitting walls everywhere and doesn't have the intellectual or spiritual equipment to deal with the resulting mess. All we can do is argue for more of the same: more onward momentum, more technological mediation, more control. Are these anything more than the fantasies of people whose worldview is crumbling? Are they any more than delusions?

Certainly many of these fantasies – because this is what

they are – start to fall apart on examination. Take that colonisation of Mars, for example. The writer John Michael Greer recently drew attention to a paper published in the journal *Nature* in 1997. A team of economists had calculated how much value was contributed to the global economy by nature, as opposed to human effort. Their results suggested that, for every US dollar's worth of goods and services consumed by human beings each year, around 75 cents are provided free of charge by the Earth's ecosystems. Only the remaining 25 cents were created by human economic activity. If we were to colonise a dead planet, like Mars, we would somehow need to make up that 75 per cent on our own, working it up from a world of dead rock and dust. How would we do it? We have no idea. In all likelihood, it would be entirely impossible.

So, what should we call this clutching at straws? We could call it idealism, even utopianism. It is clearly both of those things. But perhaps it is something else too. Perhaps it is a modern-day form of Romanticism.

Look up the word 'Romantic' in a dictionary, and you will be met with definitions like this: 'Exaggeration or picturesque falsehood . . . A sense of remoteness from or idealisation of everyday life . . . Exaggerate or distort the truth, especially fantastically'. 'Romantic' is a word that is commonly thrown around, often by the kind of people who idealise Mars bases, to dismiss people who draw inspiration from the past rather than the future. It is a popular insult, which, as so many insults do, relieves the insulter of the burden of thinking.

A 'Romantic', in these terms, is somebody who views the past through 'rose-tinted spectacles', and desires a return to it. Somebody who, for example, idealises rural communities and low-technology cultures, and doesn't understand the harshness and horror of preindustrial life. Our 'Romantic' is usually a bourgeois escapist, who sees 'nature' as welcoming rather than threatening, doesn't realise that life before the coming of antibiotics and television was nasty, brutish and short, and is able to hold those views only because of his or her privileged position within the protective bubble of industrial society.

This caricature is not entirely unfounded. Certainly there are plenty of naive visions of the past around, and there are plenty of unrealistic assessments of the present as well. But it seems to me that Romanticising the past, in our culture at this point in time, is less common than Romanticising the future. The only difference is that Romanticising the future is socially acceptable.

Consider what the two worldviews have in common. One of them looks back to a period of the past that is considered to be superior to the present, and draws inspiration from it. So a 'primitivist', for example, may look right back to the Palaeolithic era, before the development of agriculture, and hail this as the high point of human development. We lived in harmony with the natural world until the first grain seed was cultivated, after which we slid into a future of hierarchy, control and ecological destruction. Because there is no possibility of getting back to this period, and because we know very little about it, it is easy to project our emotional needs onto it. This is essentially the Christian narrative of the Fall retooled for an anti-capitalist age, and it has the same primal appeal.

It's not hard to find people who swim in these waters.

I've swum there myself, and I find it a tempting and comforting story. Perhaps buying into narratives such as this is foolish, or perhaps it is just human. But if it is foolish, is it any more so than indulging in fantasies about Moon bases and salvation by silicon chip? What is the difference between those who project their needs onto the past, and those who project them onto the future? What is the difference between someone who sees perfection in the ice age, and someone who sees perfection in the space age? It may not always be realistic to look to the past for inspiration, but at least we know, more or less, what the past was like. We have no idea what the future will bring. Perhaps that is the attraction: space is empty, in every sense, and that makes it big enough to contain all of our dreams, however baroque.

Still, if we are going to use words like 'Romantic', we should at least understand their provenance. The Romantic movement, which flourished during the first half of the nineteenth century, was a reaction to the utilitarianism of the eighteenth-century 'Enlightenment'. It responded to the dehumanising impact of mass industry, the rationalisation of nature and the increasing emphasis on human reason, with a defence of an emotional, intuitive reaction to the natural world and to human relationships. Though it is perhaps best known today through the poetry of Wordsworth or the art of the German landscape painters, it was at the time just as deeply entwined with radical politics and an assault on the dogmas of materialism and scientism. If it sometimes idealised the past, that was probably an inevitable reaction to the bombastic championing of the future that was going on all around.

Personally, I don't think the word 'Romantic' should be used as an insult at all; like its counterpart 'Luddite', it is a misused historical term. But if it must be – and perhaps it is too late to turn things around – then at least let it be an equal-opportunities insult. If it is to be used to condemn those who idealise particular time periods, let the time periods encompass those yet to come as well as those that have gone.

Looked at this way, the Mars-base future, like the future in which we rebuild passenger pigeons in laboratories, breed babies in machines and download our consciousness into silicon chips, is an exercise in space-age Romanticism. The kind of people who are disgusted by an idealised past can often barely contain their enthusiasm for an idealised future. And when objections are raised, they can dress their visions up in moral language: we must save the planet; we must provide new space for humans to develop and meet their ever-increasing needs. Expect to hear more of this in years to come, as the situation here on Earth grows more desperate.

What is to be done about this? The answer to this question, as so often, seems to me to be personal rather than political. There is no way to prevent this society from Romanticising progress and technology, and there is no way to prevent it coming down hard on visions of human-scale and ecological development. It will continue to do this until its own intellectual framework, and probably its physical framework, collapses under its own weight. These attitudes are in our space-age DNA.

But what we can do, when presented with a vision that projects an ideal onto either the future or the past, is examine our own personal need to be deluded. Engage with any of the world's great spiritual teachers, or many of its secular philosophers, and you will come across the claim that most of us, most of the time, are caught up in our own delusions. That is to say, we are creating our own mental maps of the world, by which we navigate its harsh tracts, and we are hugely reluctant to see these maps taken from us, or to see any of the directions printed on them questioned. These maps may be religious, philosophical, political or any variation of these things. But they mean that when we look out at the world, we don't see the world itself, we see our own perception of it, and that perception of it is coloured by our own emotional needs.

So, if we need to believe in progress, we will believe in progress. If we need to believe in Apocalypse, we will believe in that. If we need to deny the existence of climate change, or believe we can go back to the Pleistocene or forward to the Martian future, we will believe those things, and as long as we want to believe them, nothing can tear those maps from our hands.

The purpose of delusions is to comfort us, and our space-age delusions comfort us on a civilisational level. The best way around them is probably to examine our own mental maps – and thus our own minds – and try to deflect them as they come. This is the work of a lifetime, but perhaps in the end it is the only work.

'All that we are', explained the Buddha 2,500 years ago, 'is the result of what we have thought. The mind is everything. What we think we become.' We can see what our civilisation is becoming, and where it is going too. What delusions brought us here – and how do we begin to strip them away?

Global Oneness Project, 2013

The Quants and the Poets

If, a century ago, the keenest talking heads of the age had battled it out among themselves about the future of infrastructure and energy, what would that debate have looked like? If, say, they had all agreed on the importance of rolling out a massive, global plan stretching decades into the future, based on endlessly argued-over scientific 'facts', which themselves disguised a lot of underlying political, cultural and social assumptions about the way the world is – what would they have been arguing about? Precisely how many ostlers would be needed by 1950? The importance of a large-scale dung clean-up operation on the streets of major cities? A research and development programme to investigate the plausibility of time machines? Sourcing the funding for an urgent nationwide rollout of dirigible charging stations?

Thoughts like these have been drifting into my head, then drifting out again, in recent weeks, as I have observed the world's intellectual classes arguing furiously about nuclear energy. Not for the first time, a major nuclear accident – this time at the Fukushima plant in Japan – has focused human minds, at least for a few days, on where and how their miracle supplies of energy are produced. As usual, the result has been rancorous and almost entirely inconclusive.

I am, it is safe to say, no scientist (something I have in common with most of those who hold strong opinions on nuclear power, by the look of things) and I have no real idea what has gone on in those Japanese reactors (ditto). I don't know, either, whether the worst nuclear accident since Chernobyl will turn out to be the high-water mark of the global nuclear industry – something that would apparently be a triumph or a catastrophe depending on which pundit you're listening to.

But I do wonder whether it is a high-water mark for the environmental movement. For a long time now, the green movement has been in retreat, and that retreat now seems in danger of turning into a rout. From a standing start four decades ago, the greens have seen some of their ideas (mainly the ones about using 'our resources' 'sustainably') spread widely and sometimes deeply into popular and political culture. They have also, inevitably, seen those ideas watered down. I have covered this subject before and don't intend to do so again here in any detail, but it might be worth reflecting a little bit on the bind that the environmental movement now finds itself in, across the world.

At this point in history the all-consuming global industrial system – R. S. Thomas's 'Machine' – is effectively unstoppable; it will run on until it runs out. This Machine needs 'resources' – the products of natural systems – like a fish needs water. When the global scrabble for these resources is combined with accelerating technological change, a rising human population, the virus-like spread of consumer values, a mass-extinction event, a changing climate and resource scarcity in a number of (admittedly contested) areas, the results do not look pretty.

At this point, things get complicated. If we are highly politicised people, whose values and self-image are predicated on being 'activists' in the cause of preventing such terrible things, we may simply not allow ourselves to be honest about this. This is understandable and I know what it feels like, having been there myself for quite a long time. At this point, we have to lie to ourselves – to go into denial for the sake of our psychological health. So we might pretend to ourselves that 'one more push' (in other words, doing the same thing again) may do the trick. We might tell ourselves that The People are ignorant of The Facts and that if we enlighten them they will Act. We might believe that the right treaty has yet to be signed, or the right technology yet to be found, or that the problem is not too much growth and science and progress but too little of it. Or we might choose to believe that a Movement is needed to expose the lies being told to The People by The Bad Men In Power who are preventing The People from doing the rising up they will all want to do when they learn The Truth.

Whatever the story, it will be a story based on the need for an external event or events, which can only be brought into being by way of more 'action'. This way, we can tell ourselves that the only thing to do is to keep on keeping on. After all, the alternative must be 'giving up' and watching the world burn.

This is where the greens are today. It is a hard place to be, and it is a place made even more fearsome by the single-minded obsession with climate change that has gripped environmentalism over the last decade. The fear of carbon has trumped all other issues – so much so that is now common in popular culture to see 'green' ideas represented simply as arguments about carbon emissions. Everything else has been stripped away.

It is in this context that the nuclear rumpus has occurred.

A Japanese earthquake and tsunami ripped apart a nuclear power plant, and with barely a day's grace the pundits were swooping on the place. Most of them seemed to see this tragedy simply as an opportunity to restate forcefully their existing positions on nuclear power – It will kill us! It will save us! – even as the fuel rods were still melting. But whatever the argument, the growing – and understandable – sense of desperation was the same.

If you believe that climate change will wreck the Earth – or at least this incarnation of it – and that the only way to prevent that from happening is to 'reduce emissions' in a fantastically short time period, then you are in a very perilous place. It's not that this argument is necessarily wrong – it probably isn't, though the lack of certainty is always worth highlighting. But it is so obviously impossible to do what it is claimed Must Be Done to stop it, that futility or despair can end up being the only places to turn.

My feeling is that the green movement has torpedoed itself with numbers. Its single-minded obsession with climate change, and its insistence on seeing this as an engineering challenge, which must be overcome with technological solutions guided by the neutral gaze of Science, has forced it into a ghetto. Many popular environmentalists (if that's not a contradiction in terms) now spend their time arguing about whether they prefer windfarms to wave machines or nuclear power to carbon sequestration. They offer up remarkably confident predictions of what will happen if we do or don't do this or that, all based on mind-numbing numbers grabbed from this or that 'study' as if the world were a giant spreadsheet that needs only to be balanced correctly.

In this, the green movement is only reflecting and feeding on wider societal trends. We live in a remarkably literal-minded and reductionistic culture. I'm struck listening to or reading the news, for example, by how nothing is seen to be 'real' unless it is sanctioned by the priesthoods of either Science or Economics, and preferably both. This is the kind of culture that produces an environmental movement made up of frustrated, passionate people who feel obliged to act like speak-your-weight machines in order to be heard.

If we want to move beyond the futility and despair imposed by the cold narrowness of this worldview, where do we look? What is missing here is stories, and an understanding of the importance of stories in getting to the bottom of what is really going on. Because, at root, this whole squabble between worldviews is not about numbers at all – it is about narratives.

The fight between the pro-nukers and the anti-nukers, for example, is actually quite archetypal. Though both sides pretend to be informed by 'science' and 'facts' both are actually informed primarily by intuition and prejudice. Whether you like nuclear power or not is a reflection of the kind of worldview you have: whether you are a confident embracer of the Western model of progress or whether it frightens or concerns you; whether you trust science or tend not to; whether you are cautious or reckless; whether you are 'progressive' or 'conservative'. On issues ranging from genetically modified crops to capitalism, these are the underlying stories that inform the green debate. That they are then supported by a clutch of cherry-picked facts – easy to come by, after all, in the age of Wikipedia – is a footnote to what's really going on.

The mess that the greens have got themselves into is at

least partly due to them paying more attention to numbers than narratives. Green political thought, in its early incarnations, was radical and challenging. It was about the stories we tell ourselves about the world: stories about progress, industry, the conquest of nature and the like. The early greens challenged these stories with others, drawn in some cases from ecotopian imaginings about a better future but in many more cases from the stories of existing non-industrial societies: the Kalahari Bush People, for example, who lived for 35,000 years in a culture that managed to survive in remarkable harmony with non-human nature, even with lions prowling around the huts of its people. You want 'sustainability'? The Bush People were the longest-recorded human culture. They were genuinely sustainable for longer than we can imagine. Industrial society got them in the end, like it gets everything, but the example remains.

This kind of thing, of course, was what made it so easy to attack environmentalists as Romantics and primitivists (which some of them were and still are). In response, environmentalists decided to get 'serious', so as to be listened to in the corridors of power. They started wearing suits and pretending to be economists and speaking the language of business and science. It was a perfectly sensible approach – the only approach, if they wanted to be heard by the power-brokers – and it yielded many clear dividends.

But it may also have doomed the greens in the longer term, for now they find themselves caught in a narrative of other people's making. Almost by accident, mainstream green politics and argument threw out most of the alternative stories it grew up with, like a child throws out his old teddy bears: that was then, but this is now, and now we are

Grown-Ups. This approach has left environmentalism in a position where its advocates now find themselves unable to do anything but argue about which machines they would prefer to use to power an ever-growing industrial economy. Any sally outside this tightly controlled ghetto sees them rained with bullets from all sides: accused of wishful thinking if they talk about zero-growth economies; called snobs and hypocrites if they criticise consumerism; attacked as terrorists if they engage in direct action to protect wild nature; called naive idealists if they ask whether planning for a future much like the present is really such a good idea.

This has always been the case, of course, but now the greens are being heard in the corridors of power the stakes are much higher. A global anti-green movement now exists and is growing in power and influence. Meanwhile, a once challenging movement has been taken over from within by smooth-tongued purveyors of business-as-usual without the carbon. The message is clear: stick to arguing about the machines, and you're welcome to play with the big boys. But drop all the other nonsense, OK? This, demonstrably, is how radical movements die.

I'm currently trying to get my head around exactly how the 2008 economic collapse happened, and in the cause of doing so I am reading John Lanchester's book *Whoops!*, which explains it in terms that even people like me can grasp. This evening I was reading Lanchester's description of how banks have changed in the last few decades. When the author's father worked in banking, it was a staid business populated mostly by non-graduates. Today, if you don't have a first-class maths degree from Oxbridge or an Ivy League university, you'll find it hard making it in the industry. This, Lanchester suggests, is part of the problem: banking has become so specialist, so complex, that most people – including many bankers – simply don't understand how it works.

The maths geeks who now run the futures and options operations in banking are known as 'quants'. One MBA student quoted in the book reported that on his course the students were required to identify themselves as either 'quants' or 'poets'. That is: did they do numbers, or did they do words?

These days, the green movement is being taken over by quants. It's easy to see why. Quants present easy, numbered, labelled arguments which may sometimes require a maths degree but don't require a rewiring of your worldview or an examination of your narrative. A green quant might be telling you to change your lightbulbs or come out on the streets in favour of a nuclear power plant or a windfarm, but he's not asking you to examine your values or your society's underlying mythology. And if you talk to him about this, it is very easy indeed for him to laugh and tell you loftily that this is all very nice but is hardly comparable to the serious business of saving the world one emission at a time.

This is the context in which the nuclear squabble is being played out. I recently read, for example, an article that claimed that renewable energy can't meet 'our energy needs'. But our needs for what? Coffee machines and fast broadband, or clean drinking water and living ecosystems? Middle-class life in a consumer democracy or a liveable human existence? Or do we now think these are the same thing? If you really want to see where a green quant is coming from, simply catch him in the middle of one of these arguments and ask him (and it usually is a him) to define 'need'. Then watch the narrative spooling out like film from a broken canister.

As a poet, of course, I have a vested interest in objecting to this, and I often do, but I don't do it without empathy or without some doubt. I know why it has happened. This, after all, is an approach designed to produce clear and concrete results – something that is undeniably useful in an age of ecocide. But what narrative framework are the results being produced in? Because it's that framework, in the end, that will determine where those results take us.

Too many green quants, then, and not enough green poets? I think so. Or rather, I think that the poets have been cowed into silence by the dominance and urgency of the quants' narrative. How to reassert the importance of stories, then, is perhaps a key question now. Green poets might perhaps start by observing that worlds are not 'saved' by the same stories that are killing them. They might want to observe that saving worlds is an impossible business in the first place. Or they might try to explore what it is about how we see ourselves that reduces us to this, time and time again – arguing about machines rather than wondering what those machines give us and what they take away.

The friction between the quant and the poet could be represented by focusing on a few bickering individuals, or by trying to divide the greens up into Two Cultures. But it could also, perhaps more honestly and productively, be represented as a tension that is present within all of us. None of us is wholly, or even primarily, rational and analytical, and none of us is quite devoid of poetry either, though it is sometimes hard to find it.

These divisions are themselves stories that we, in this particular culture, tell ourselves about how humans work. The quants and the poets are both needed, but I would argue that, right now, the poets ought to take the lead – if indeed that is ever something that poets are capable of. We have no shortage of arguments about numbers and machines, but we do have a great shortage of workable stories. That is to say: stories that don't just have happy endings, but have convincing plots as well.

dark-mountain.net, 2011

A Short History of Loss

Thoughts on Biophilia

In October 2006, a beekeeper from Pennsylvania in the United States dropped off 400 colonies of bees in Florida, to overwinter in the much warmer state. A month later, when he returned to check on his hives, he was bewildered to find that most of the bees were missing. The queens were still there, and some of the young, but all of the older bees – the honeybees, who went out foraging for nectar and brought it back to feed the hive – had completely disappeared. The collapse had been rapid and almost total: only 9 of his 400 colonies remained intact.

Beekeepers regularly experience the loss of some colonies, and bees are often killed by parasites, cold winters and other natural phenomena. But this was different. Over the next six months, nearly a quarter of all the beekeepers across the US experienced similar disappearances, losing nearly half of all their hives. Every year since then, the problem has escalated: by 2013, around half of all the honeybee hives in the United States were victims of this new and mysterious plague.

Soon the problem spread further and 'colony collapse disorder', as the phenomenon became known, was experienced across Europe too. Between 2008 and 2013, the honeybee population was reported to have dropped by 30 per cent in

Britain, 40 per cent in Italy and Germany and 50 per cent in Switzerland. If the collapse continues, the bee problem could become a human problem: many of our crops rely on bees and other insects to pollinate them.

In May 2014, a report by Harvard University biologists claimed to have identified the cause of the bee collapse: a relatively new kind of pesticide known as a neonicotinoid. When colonies were deliberately treated with these pesticides, the honeybees within would abandon their hives and not return. The scientists suggested that the pesticides might be impairing the bees' memory or brain functions, making them unable to fully function, or to remember their way home.

Fortunately, over in another department of Harvard University, another team of scientists was working on a project that might render honeybees ultimately replaceable. The 'Robobees' project, run by the School of Engineering and Applied Sciences, is dedicated, as the name suggests, to building robotic bees. In 2009, in response to the news about colony collapse disorder, one of the team explained that they 'began to seriously consider what it would take to create a robotic bee colony. We wondered if mechanical bees could replicate not just an individual's behaviour but the unique behaviour that emerges out of interactions among thousands of bees.'

So far, the Robobees team has succeeded in creating bee-sized robots and making them fly. The next step is to make them cooperate like a real hive. After that, the robotic insects may be trained to pollinate plants or even to work as part of search-and-rescue operations in disaster zones. The Robobees scientists are keen to stress that they don't want their creations to replace real bees, but many of their supporters are not so shy about the ultimate endpoint of the project. The Robobees project 'might seem unsettling, and a violation of our aesthetic sensibilities', explained one futurist web magazine, 'but we'd essentially be replacing biological "robots" with synthetic ones'.

How did we get to the point where we regard a living creature as a 'robot': and an inefficient one at that, ripe for replacement with better models once we have worked out how to make them? What errors have led us to this way of seeing? Were they the same errors that got us to the point where we were both willing and able to spray landscapes with toxic pesticides that wipe out vast swathes of insect life? Were they the same errors that could change the climate of an entire planet, trigger a sixth mass-extinction event, acidify oceans, break up ice caps and shred the last great wild forests and their inhabitants in the cause of toilet paper and soya mince?

We live in what is easily the most ecologically destructive culture in human history. But how did we get here? Have humans always been hardwired for ecocide, or did things go wrong somewhere along the journey? Was there an event, or a series of events, in our history that led us to the point where we regarded ourselves as separate from something external called 'nature', which we could choose either to idealise for pleasure or ravage for profit? If so, can we identify and learn from them?

The notion that humankind has experienced a Fall – a point at which we were ejected from a prelapsarian garden – runs like a golden thread through Western culture. In his novel *Ishmael*, Daniel Quinn suggests that the biblical story of the Fall is a dim historical memory: a retelling through myth of the human development of agriculture.

The Garden of Eden represents the prehistoric world of the hunter-gatherer tribes who were displaced by agriculturalists. The development of agriculture, far from being a leap forward, was in this reading a disaster. People were forced to leave a world in which wild creatures were abundant, hunting was relatively easy and edible food was widespread, for backbreaking toil in the fields, a shorter and less healthy life, and a constant battle to subdue nature with ploughs and walls and fences and flocks.

Perhaps, then, the development of agriculture, which is the basis for all modern civilisations, was the point at which we began to look at the non-human world as a collection of potential resources to be utilised, rather than as a community to which we belonged. Certainly it was the development of agriculture, and the settled communities, towns and eventually cities that resulted, that allowed us to create the hierarchical, technologically dependent global civilisation that today is denuding the planet of its riches.

Perhaps, on the other hand, the problem is not agriculture but industry. Until the Industrial Revolution really got off the ground in the eighteenth century, the Earth's human population was small and relatively limited in the damage it could do. Then we discovered and began to extract and burn coal, gas and oil, and the party really began. It could be that the climate change that this most recent of technological leaps has already set in motion will knock the human experiment with civilisation on the head altogether. It is too early to say.

Then again, perhaps the problem goes much further back than this. Perhaps the taming of fire by human beings was the point at which we separated ourselves from other creatures. Perhaps it was the making of tools, which allowed us to hunt and kill way beyond the level that might be considered 'natural'. The novelist William Golding believed that the development of language itself represented a symbolic break in human evolution: language, he suggested, allowed us to overlay abstractions onto reality and begin to shift away from that reality into our self-created internal universe.

In reality, there was probably no one moment before which we lived in harmony and after which a covenant was broken. Instead, there is a historical arc that can be traced from the development of human language to the development of synthetic bees. If there is, in the words of Thor Heyerdahl, 'nothing for modern man to return to', the question is what we can move on to, and how we can do it in a way that brings us back in tune with what the philosopher Thomas Berry called 'the great conversation' between humans and the rest of the natural world.

Certainly that conversation is almost non-existent in the modern West today. The twenty-first century is shaping up to be the age in which post-Enlightenment humanity finally realises a long-cherished ambition: to rebuild the planet in its own image. Probably we have been doing this since we planted the first seeds and bred the first livestock, but we have the power now to take things to a whole new level: to modify the genes of plants and animals, to build robotic alternatives to living creatures and to use the techniques of synthetic biology to create new living creatures from scratch, which can be sent out into the world with the sole purpose of achieving a human end. For centuries we have dreamt of usurping the gods. Many would like to believe that it is about to happen.

The increasingly fashionable word 'biophilia' seems to me to be simply a modern, science-sanctioned way of describing a very ancient kind of love: a love for the natural world of which we are part. 'Nature' is not something external to us, it is something we are part of and something that is within us: what are we if not natural? 'Biophilia', then – love of life – is as natural as love of your wife or husband or children or parents. Your relationship with nature may sometimes be as difficult and stormy as your relationship with any of them, but none of these relationships can ever go away, and they all change you. We are all bound up together. Watch any child play in a field or wood: they know this. Then they – we – grow up and learn to convince themselves that 'objective' reality is somehow different from lived experience. We learn to convince ourselves that the world is a machine, not an animal, that it is unconscious and meaningless and that the only questions to be asked are questions of *how* and not questions of *why* or *whether.*

However we got here, we have managed to create a culture in which we have alienated ourselves from the rest of life. We struggle to persuade ourselves that this alienation is the same thing as freedom. Increasingly, though, for those penned into cities with no view of the stars and no taste of clean air and nothing but grass between the cracks in the pavement to nourish their sense of the wild, this is no freedom at all. We have made ourselves caged animals, and all the gadgets in the world cannot compensate for what we have lost.

Humans are animals – undomesticated animals – and there is something in us that still yearns for that great conversation. We need it, as we need water and air and food. Often this sense of a need to connect with wild nature is mocked or belittled in contemporary culture: dismissed as romantic, backward-looking, naive, irrelevant to the serious business of living in the 'modern world'. In reality, it is that modern world that is out of tune with what sings in the human body. Biophilia is as natural and inherent as any other form of human love, and it is not going away. All the Robobees and artificial forests on Earth cannot make up for our strange, strong sense that living without wild nature is like living without one of our senses or one of our limbs.

As the Christians have their story of a Fall from a prehistoric Eden, the Hindus have a belief that the world travels through four different ages, or *yugas*. The age we are currently living in is the *Kali yuga*: a dark age characterised by degeneration and greed. Avarice and a general disrespect for life define the *kali yuga:* it is the age when humans have been telling themselves that they are equal to the gods for so long that they begin to believe it and act on it, with catastrophic consequences.

Only when this era is over, Hindu mythology tells us, will sanity begin to prevail again. But in the decline of one age, and one way of seeing, there is always contained the seed of another. If an unexamined yearning to reconnect with the wild world remains within us, then perhaps we will never quite allow ourselves to be tamed. It is a delicious thought that what might save us, in the end, will not be a new economic arrangement or a new politics or another revolution or a series of wonder technologies, but our own inner wildness, pushed under so hard and for so long that it finally bursts to the surface again, hungry for what it has lost.

Biophilia, 2015

II : WITHDRAWAL

Confessions of a Recovering Environmentalist

> Some See Nature all Ridicule & Deformity . . . & Some Scarce see Nature at all. But to the Eyes of the Man of Imagination, Nature is Imagination itself.
> *William Blake*

SCENES FROM A YOUNGER LIFE 1

I am twelve years old. I am alone, I am scared, I am cold and I am crying my eyes out. I can't see more than six feet in either direction. I am on some godforsaken moor high up on the dark, ancient, poisonous spine of England. The black bog juice I have been trudging through for hours has long since crept over the tops of my boots and down into my socks. My rucksack is too heavy, I am unloved and lost and I will never find my way home. It is raining and the cloud is punishing me; clinging to me, laughing at me. Twenty-five years later, I still have a felt memory of that experience and its emotions: a real despair and a terrible loneliness.

I do find my way home; I manage to keep to the path and eventually catch up with my father, who has the map and the compass and the mini Mars bars. He was always there, somewhere up ahead, but he had decided it would be good for me to 'learn to keep up' with him. All of this, he tells me, will make me into a man.

61

Only later do I realise the complexity of the emotions summoned by a childhood laced with experiences like this. My father was a compulsive long-distance walker. Every year, throughout my most formative decade, he would take me away to Cumbria or Northumberland or Yorkshire or Cornwall or Pembrokeshire or the Welsh Marches, and we would walk, for weeks. We would follow ancient tracks or new trails, across mountains and moors and ebony black cliffs. Much of the time we would be alone with each other and with our thoughts and our conversations, and we would be alone with the oystercatchers, the gannets, the curlews, the skylarks and the owls. With the gale and the breeze, with our maps and compasses and emergency rations and bivvy bags and plastic bottles of water. We would camp in the heather, by cairns and old mine shafts, hundreds of feet above the orange lights of civilisation, and I would dream. And in the morning, with dew on the tent and cold air in my face as I opened the zip, the wild elements of life, all of the real things, would all seem to be there, waiting for me with the sunrise.

SCENES FROM A YOUNGER LIFE 2

I am nineteen years old. It is around midnight and I am on the summit of a low, chalk down, the last of the long chain that winds its way through the crowded, peopled, fractious South Country. There are maybe fifty or sixty people there with me. There is a fire going, there are guitars, there is singing and there are weird and unnerving whooping noises from some of the ragged travellers who have made this place their home.

This is Twyford Down, a hilltop east of Winchester. There is something powerful about this place; something ancient and unanswering. Soon it is to be destroyed: a six-lane motorway will be driven through it in a deep chalk cutting. It is vital that this should happen in order to reduce the journey time of travellers between London and Southampton by a full thirteen minutes. The people up here have made it their home in a doomed attempt to stop this happening.

From outside it is impossible to see, and most do not want to. The name-calling has been going on for months, in the papers and the pubs and in the House of Commons. The people here are Luddites, nimbies, reactionaries, romantics. They are standing in the way of progress. They will not be tolerated. Inside, there is a sense of shared threat and solidarity, there are blocks of hash and packets of Rizlas and litres of bad cider. We know what we are here for. We know what we are doing. We can feel the reason in the soil and in the night air. Down there, under the lights and behind the curtains, there is no chance that they will ever understand. We are on our own.

Someone I don't know suggests we dance the maze. Out beyond the firelight, there is a maze carved into the down's soft, chalk turf. I don't know if it's some ancient monument or a new creation. Either way, it's the same spiral pattern that can be found carved in rocks from millennia ago. With cans and cigarettes and spliffs in our hands, a small group of us starts to walk the maze, laughing, staggering, then breaking into a run, singing, spluttering, stumbling together towards the centre.

SCENES FROM A YOUNGER LIFE 3

I am twenty-one years old and I've just spent the most exciting two months of my life so far in an Indonesian rainforest. I've just been on one of those organised expeditions
that people of my age buy into to give them the chance to
do something useful and exciting in what used to be called
the 'Third World'. I've prepared for months for this. I've
sold double glazing door to door to scrape the cash together.
I have been reading Bruce Chatwin and Redmond O'Han-
lon and Benedict Allen and my head is full of magic and
idiocy and wonder.

During my trip, there were plenty of all of these things.
I still vividly remember klotok journeys up Borneo rivers
by moonlight, watching the swarms of giant fruitbats overhead. I remember the hooting of gibbons and the search for
hornbills high up in the rainforest canopy. I remember a
four-day trek through a so-called 'rain' forest that was so
dry we ended up drinking filtered mud. I remember tur-
tle eggs on the beaches of Java and young orang-utans at
the rehabilitation centre where we worked in Kalimantan,
sitting in the high branches of trees with people's stolen
underpants on their heads, laughing at us. I remember the
gold miners and the loggers, and the freshwater crocodiles
in the same river we swam in every morning. I remember
my first sight of flying fish in the Java Sea.

And I remember the small islands north of Lombok where
some of us spent a few days before we came home. At night
we would go down to the moonlit beach, where the sea and
the air would still be warm, and in the sea were millions of
tiny lights: phosphorescence. I had never seen this before;

never even heard of it. We would walk into the water and immerse ourselves and rise up again and the lights would cling to our bodies, fading away as we laughed.

Now, back home, the world seems changed. A two-month break from my country, my upbringing, my cultural assumptions, a two-month immersion in something far more raw and unmediated, has left me open to seeing this place as it really is. I see the atomisation and the inward focus and the faces of the people in a hurry on the other side of windscreens. I see the streetlights and the asphalt as I had not quite seen them before. What I see most of all are the adverts.

For the first time, I realise the extent and the scope and the impacts of the billboards, the posters, the TV and radio ads. Everywhere an image, a phrase, a demand or a recommendation is screaming for my attention, trying to sell me something, tell me who to be, what to desire and to need. And this is before the internet; before Apples and BlackBerries became indispensable to people who wouldn't know where to pick the real thing; before the deep, accelerating immersion of people in their technologies, even outdoors, even in the sunshine. Compared to where I have been, this world is so tamed, so mediated and commoditised, that something within it seems to have broken off and been lost beneath the slabs. No one has noticed this, or says so if they have. Something is missing: I can almost see the gap where it used to be. But it is not remarked upon. Nobody says a thing.

*

It is 9.30 at night in mid-December at the end of the first decade of the twenty-first century. I step outside my front door into the farmyard and I walk over to the track, letting my eyes adjust to the dark. I am lucky enough to be living among the Cumbrian fells now, and as my pupils widen I can see, under a clear, starlit sky, the outline of the Old Man of Coniston, Dow Crag, Wetherlam, Helvellyn, the Fairfield Horseshoe. I stand for ten minutes, growing colder. I see two shooting stars and a satellite. I suddenly wish my dad was still alive, and I wonder where the magic has gone.

These experiences, and others like them, were what formed me. They were what made me what I would later learn to call an 'environmentalist': something that seemed rebellious and excitingly outsiderish when I first took it up (and which successfully horrified my social-climbing father, especially as it was partly his fault) but which these days is almost de rigueur among the British bourgeoisie. Early in my adult life, just after I came back from Twyford Down, I vowed, self-importantly, that this would be my life's work: saving nature from people. Preventing the destruction of beauty and brilliance, speaking up for the small and the overlooked and the things that could not speak for themselves. When I look back on this now, I'm quite touched by my younger self. I would like to be him again, perhaps just for a day; someone to whom all sensations are fiery and all answers are simple.

All of this – the downs, the woods, the rainforest, the great oceans and, perhaps most of all, the silent isolation of the moors and mountains, which at the time seemed so hateful and unremitting – took hold of me somewhere unexamined. The relief I used to feel on those long trudges with my dad when I saw the lights of a village or a remote pub, even a minor road or a pylon; any sign of humanity – as I grow older this is replaced by the relief of escaping from the towns and the villages, away from the pylons and the pubs and the people, up onto the moors again, where only the ghosts and the saucer-eyed dogs and the old legends and the wind can possess me.

But they are harder to find now, those spirits. I look out across the moonlit Lake District ranges and it's as clear as the night air that what used to come in regular waves, pounding like the sea, comes now only in flashes, out of the corner of my eyes, like a lighthouse in a storm. Perhaps it's the way the world has changed. There are more cars on the roads now, more satellites in the sky. The footpaths up the fells are like stone motorways; there are turbines on the moors and the farmers are being edged out by south country refugees like me, trying to escape but bringing with us the things we flee from. The new world is online and loving it, the virtual happily edging out the actual. The darkness is shut out and the night grows lighter and nobody is there to see it.

It could be all that, but it probably isn't. It's probably me. I am thirty-seven now. The world is smaller, more tired, more fragile, more horribly complex and full of troubles. Or, rather: the world is the same as it ever was, but I am more aware of it and of the reality of my place within it. I have grown up, and there is nothing to be done about it. The worst part of it is that I can't seem to look without thinking any more. And now I know far more about what we are do-ing. We: the people. I know what we are doing, all over the world, to everything, all of the time. I know why the magic is dying. It's me. It's us.

*

I became an 'environmentalist' because of a strong emotional reaction to wild places and the world beyond the human: to beech trees and hedgerows and pounding waterfalls, to songbirds and sunsets, to the flying fish in the Java Sea and the canopy of the rainforest at dusk when the gibbons come to the waterside to feed. From that reaction came a feeling, which became a series of thoughts: that such things are precious for their own sake, that they are food for the human soul and that they need people to speak for them to, and defend them from, other people, because they cannot speak our language and we have forgotten how to speak theirs. And because we are killing them to feed ourselves and we know it and we care about it, sometimes, but we do it anyway because we are hungry, or we have persuaded ourselves that we are.

But these are not, I think, very common views today. Today's environmentalism is as much a victim of the contemporary cult of utility as every other aspect of our lives, from science to education. We are not environmentalists now because we have an emotional reaction to the wild world. In this country, most of us wouldn't even know where to find it. We are environmentalists now in order to promote something called 'sustainability'. What does this curious, plastic word mean? It does not mean defending the non-human world from the ever-expanding empire of *Homo sapiens sapiens*, though some of its adherents like to pretend it does, even to themselves. It means sustaining human civilisation at the comfort level that the world's rich people – us – feel is their right, without destroying the 'natural capital' or the 'resource base' that is needed to do so.

It is, in other words, an entirely human-centred piece of politicking, disguised as concern for 'the planet'. In a very short time – just over a decade – this worldview has become all-pervasive. It is voiced by the president of the USA and the president of Anglo-Dutch Shell and many people in between. The success of environmentalism has been total – at the price of its soul.

Let me offer up just one example of how this pact has worked. If 'sustainability' is about anything, it is about carbon. Carbon and climate change. To listen to most environmentalists today, you would think that these were the only things in the world worth talking about. The business of 'sustainability' is the business of preventing carbon emissions. Carbon emissions threaten a potentially massive downgrading of our prospects for material advancement as a species. They threaten an unacceptable erosion of our resource base and put at risk our vital hoards of natural capital. If we cannot sort this out quickly, we are going to end up darning our socks again and growing our own carrots and holidaying in Weston-super-Mare and other such unthinkable things. All of the horrors our grandparents left behind will return like deathless legends. Carbon emissions must be 'tackled' like a drunk with a broken bottle: quickly, and with maximum force.

Don't get me wrong: I don't doubt the potency of climate change to undermine the human machine. It looks to me as if it is already beginning to do so, and that it is too late to do anything but attempt to mitigate the worst effects. But what I am also convinced of is that the fear of losing both the comfort and the meaning that our civilisation gifts us has gone to the heads of environmentalists to such a degree that they have forgotten everything else. The carbon must be stopped, like the Umayyad at Tours, or all will be lost.

This reductive approach to the human-environmental

challenge leads to an obvious conclusion: if carbon is the problem, then 'zero carbon' is the solution. Society needs to go about its business without spewing the stuff out. It needs to do this quickly, and by any means necessary. Build enough of the right kind of energy technologies, quickly enough, to generate the power we 'need' without producing greenhouse gases and there will be no need to ever turn the lights off; no need to ever slow down.

To do this will require the large-scale harvesting of the planet's ambient energy: sunlight, wind, water power. This means that vast new conglomerations of human industry are going to appear in places where this energy is most abundant. Unfortunately, these places coincide with some of the world's wildest, most beautiful and most untouched landscapes. The sort of places that environmentalism came into being to protect.

And so the deserts, perhaps the landscape always most resistant to permanent human conquest, are to be colonised by vast 'solar arrays', glass and steel and aluminium, the size of small countries. The mountains and moors, the wild uplands, are to be staked out like vampires in the sun, their chests pierced with rows of 500-foot wind turbines and associated access roads, masts, pylons and wires. The open oceans, already swimming in our plastic refuse and emptying of marine life, will be home to enormous offshore turbine ranges and hundreds of wave machines strung around the coastlines like Victorian necklaces. The rivers are to see their estuaries severed and silted by industrial barrages. The croplands and even the rainforests, the richest habitats on this terrestrial Earth, are already highly profitable sites for biofuel plantations designed to provide guilt-free car fuel to the motion-hungry masses of Europe and America.

What this adds up to should be clear enough, yet many people who should know better choose not to see it. This is business as usual: the expansive, colonising, progressive human narrative, shorn only of the carbon. It is the latest phase of our careless, self-absorbed, ambition-addled destruction of the wild, the unpolluted and the non-human. It is the mass destruction of the world's remaining wild places in order to feed the human economy. And without any sense of irony, people are calling this 'environmentalism'.

A while back I wrote an article in a newspaper highlighting the impact of industrial wind-power stations (which are usually referred to, in a nice Orwellian touch, as wind 'farms') on the uplands of Britain. I was emailed the next day by an environmentalist friend who told me he hoped I was feeling ashamed of myself. I was wrong; worse, I was dangerous. What was I doing giving succour to the fossil-fuel industry? Didn't I know that climate change would do far more damage to upland landscapes than turbines? Didn't I know that this was the only way to meet our urgent carbon targets? Didn't I see how beautiful turbines were? So much more beautiful than nuclear power stations. I might think that a 'view' was more important than the future of the entire world, but this was because I was a middle-class escapist who needed to get real.

It became apparent at that point that what I saw as the next phase of the human attack on the non-human world a lot of my environmentalist friends saw as 'progressive', 'sustainable' and 'green'. What I called destruction they called 'large-scale solutions'. This stuff was realistic, necessarily urgent. It went with the grain of human nature and the market, which as we now know are the same thing. We didn't have time to 'romanticise' the woods and the hills. There were emissions to reduce, and the end justified the means.

It took me a while to realise where this kind of talk took me back to: the maze and the moonlit hilltop. This desperate scrabble for 'sustainable development' – in reality it was the same old same old. People I had thought were on my side were arguing aggressively for the industrialising of wild places in the name of human desire. This was the same rootless, distant destruction that had led me to the top of Twyford Down. Only now there seemed to be some kind of crude equation at work that allowed them to believe this was something entirely different. Motorway through downland: bad. Wind power station on downland: good. Container port wiping out estuary mudflats: bad. Renewable hydro-power barrage wiping out estuary mudflats: good. Destruction minus carbon equals sustainability.

So here I was again: a Luddite, a nimby, a reactionary, a romantic; standing in the way of progress. I realised that I was dealing with environmentalists with no attachment to any actual environment. Their talk was of parts per million of carbon, peer-reviewed papers, sustainable technologies, renewable supergrids, green growth and the fifteenth conference of the parties. There were campaigns about 'the planet' and 'the Earth', but there was no specificity: no sign of any real, felt attachment to any small part of that Earth.

*

Back at university, in love with my newfound radicalism, as students tend to be, I started to read things. Not the stuff

I was supposed to be reading about Lollards and Wycliffe and pre-Reformation Europe, but green political thought: wild ideas I had never come across before. I could feel my mind levering itself open. Most exciting to me were the implications of a new word I stumbled across: ecocentrism. This word crystallised everything I had been feeling for years. I had no idea there were words for it or that other people felt it too, or had written intimidating books about it. The nearest I had come to such a realisation thus far was reading Wordsworth in the sixth form and feeling an excited tingling sensation as I began to understand what he was getting at among all those poems about shepherds and girls called Lucy. Here was a kindred spirit! Here was a man moved to love and fear by mountains, who believed rocks had souls, that 'Nature never did betray/The heart that loved her' (though even then that sounded a little optimistic to me). Pantheism was my new word that year.

Now I declared, to myself if no one else, that I was 'ecocentric' too. This was not the same as being egocentric, though some disagreed, and though it sounded a bit too much like 'eccentric' this was also a distraction. I was ecocentric because I did not believe – had never believed, I didn't think – that humans were the centre of the world, that the Earth was their playground, that they had the right to do what they liked or even that what they did was that important. I thought we were part of something bigger, which had as much right to the world as we did and which we were stomping on for our own benefit. I had always been haunted by shameful thoughts like this. It had always seemed to me that the beauty to be found on the trunk of a birch tree was worth any number of *Mona Lisas*, and that a Saturday-night sunset was better than Saturday-night telly. It had always seemed that most of what mattered to me could not be counted or corralled by the kind of people who thought, and still think, that I just needed to grow up.

It had been made clear to me for a long time that these feelings were at best charmingly naive and at worst backward and dangerous. Later, the dismissals became encrusted with familiar words, designed to keep the ship of human destiny afloat: romantic, Luddite, nimby and the like. For now, though, I had found my place. I was a young, fiery, radical, ecocentric environmentalist and I was going to save the world.

When I look back on the road protests of the mid-1990s, which I often do, it is with nostalgia and fondness and a sense of gratitude that I was able to be there, to see what I saw and do what I did. But I realise now that it is more than this that makes me think and talk and write about Twyford Down and Newbury and Solsbury Hill to an extent that bores even my patient friends. This, I think, was the last time I was part of an environmental movement that was genuinely environmental. The people involved were, like me, ecocentric: they didn't see 'the environment' as something 'out there'; separate from people, to be utilised or destroyed or protected according to human whim. They saw themselves as part of it, within it, of it.

There was a Wordsworthian feel to the whole thing: the defence of the trees simply because they were trees. Living under the stars and in the rain, in the oaks and in the chaotic, miraculous tunnels beneath them, in the soil itself like the rabbits and the badgers. We were connected to a place; a real place that we loved and had made a choice to belong to, if only for a short time. There was little theory, much action but even more simple being. Being in a place, knowing it, standing up for it. It was environmentalism at its rawest, and the people who came to be part of it were those who loved the land, in their hearts as well as their heads.

In years to come, this was worn away. It took a while before I started to notice what was happening, but when I did it was all around me. The ecocentrism – in simple language, the love of place, the humility, the sense of belonging, the feelings – was absent from most of the 'environmentalist' talk I heard around me. Replacing it were two other kinds of talk. One was the save-the-world-with-windfarms narrative; the same old face in new make-up. The other was a distant, sombre sound: the marching boots and rattling swords of an approaching fifth column.

Environmentalism, which in its raw, early form had no time for the encrusted, seized-up politics of left and right, offering instead a worldview that saw the growth economy and the industrialist mentality beloved by both as the problem in itself, was being sucked into the yawning, bottomless chasm of the 'progressive' left. Suddenly people like me, talking about birch trees and hilltops and sunsets, were politely, or less politely, elbowed to one side by people who were bringing a 'class analysis' to green politics.

All this talk of nature, it turned out, was bourgeois, Western and unproductive. It was a middle-class conceit, and there was nothing worse than a middle-class conceit. The workers had no time for thoughts like this (though no one bothered to notify the workers themselves that they were simply clodhopping, nature-loathing cannon fodder in a political flame war). It was terribly, objectively right wing.

Hitler liked nature after all. He was a vegetarian too. It was all deeply 'problematic'.

More problematic for me was what this kind of talk represented. With the near global failure of the left-wing project over the past few decades, green politics was fast becoming a refuge for disillusioned socialists, Trots, Marxists and a ragbag of fellow travellers who could no longer believe in communism or the Labour Party or even George Galloway, and who saw in green politics a promising bolt-hole. In they all trooped, with their Stop-the-War banners and their Palestinian-solidarity scarves, and with them they brought a new sensibility.

Now it seemed that environmentalism was not about wildness or ecocentrism or the other-than-human world and our relationship to it. Instead it was about (human) social justice and (human) equality and (human) progress and ensuring that all these things could be realised without degrading the (human) resource base that we used to call nature back when we were being naive and problematic. Suddenly, never-ending economic growth was a good thing after all: the poor needed it to get rich, which was their right. To square the circle, for those who still realised there was a circle, we were told that '(human) social justice and environmental justice go hand in hand' – a suggestion of such bizarre inaccuracy that it could surely only be wishful thinking.

Suddenly, sustaining a global human population of 10 billion people was not a problem at all, and anyone who suggested otherwise was not highlighting any obvious ecological crunch points but was giving succour to fascism or racism or gender discrimination or orientalism or essentialism or some other such hip and largely unexamined concept.

The 'real issue', it seemed, was not the human relationship with the non-human world; it was fat cats and bankers and cap'lism. These things must be destroyed, by way of marches, protests and votes for fringe political parties, to make way for something known as 'eco-socialism': a conflation of concepts that pretty much guarantees the instant hostility of 95 per cent of the population.

I didn't object to this because I thought that environmentalism should occupy the right rather than the left wing, or because I was right wing myself, which I wasn't (these days I tend to consider the entire bird with a kind of frustrated detachment). And I understood that there was at least a partial reason for the success of this colonisation of the greens by the reds. Modern environmentalism sprang partly from the early twentieth-century conservation movement, and that movement had often been about preserving supposedly pristine landscapes at the expense of people. Forcing tribal people from their ancestral lands, which had been newly designated as national parks, for example, in order to create a fictional 'untouched nature' had once been fairly common, from Africa to the US. And actually, Hitler had been something of an environmentalist, and the wellsprings that nourished some green thought nourished the thought of some other unsavoury characters too (a fact that some ideologues love to point to when witch-hunting the greens, as if it wouldn't be just as easy to point out that ideas of equality and 'social justice' fuelled Stalin and Pol Pot).

In this context it was fine to make it clear that environmentalism allied itself with ideas of justice and decency, and that it was about people as well as everything else on the planet. Of course it was, for 'nature' as something separate from people has never existed. We are nature, and the environmentalist project was always supposed to be about how we are to be part of it, to live well as part of it, to understand and respect it, to understand our place within it and to feel it as part of ourselves.

So there was a reason for environmentalism's shift to the left, just as there was a reason for its blinding obsession with carbon. Meanwhile, the fact of what humans are doing to the world had become so obvious, even to those who were doing very well out of it, that it became hard not to listen to the greens. Success duly arrived. You can't open a newspaper now or visit a corporate website or listen to a politician or read the label on a packet of biscuits without being bombarded with propaganda about the importance of 'saving the planet'. But there is a terrible hollowness to it all; a sense that society is going through the motions without understanding why. The shift, the pact, has come at a probably fatal price.

Now that price is being paid. The weird and unintentional pincer movement of the failed left, with its class analysis of waterfalls and fresh air, and the managerial, carbon-*über-alles* brigade has infiltrated, ironed out and reworked environmentalism for its own ends. Now it is not about the ridiculous beauty of coral, the mist over the fields at dawn. It is not about ecocentrism. It is not about reforging a connection between over-civilised people and the world outside their windows. It is not about living close to the land or valuing the world for the sake of the world. It is not about attacking the self-absorbed conceits of the bubble that our civilisation has become.

Today's environmentalism is about people. It is a consolation prize for a gaggle of washed-up Trots and at the same time, with an amusing irony, it is an adjunct to hyper-capitalism; the catalytic converter on the silver SUV of the global economy. It is an engineering challenge; a problem-solving device for people to whom the sight of a wild Pennine hilltop on a clear winter day brings not feelings of transcendence but thoughts about the wasted potential for renewable energy. It is about saving civilisation from the results of its own actions; a desperate attempt to prevent Gaia from hiccupping and wiping out our coffee shops and broadband connections. It is our last hope.

*

I generalise, of course. Environmentalism's chancel is as accommodating as that of socialism, anarchism or conservatism, and just as capable of generating poisonous internal bickering that will last until the death of the sun. Many who call themselves green have little time for the mainstream line I am attacking here. But it is the mainstream line. It is how most people see environmentalism today, even if it is not how all environmentalists intend it to be seen. These are the arguments and the positions that popular environmentalism – now a global force – offers up in its quest for redemption. There are reasons; there are always reasons. But whatever they are, they have led the greens down a dark, litter-strewn dead-end street, where the bins overflow, the lightbulbs have blown and the stray dogs are very hungry indeed.

What is to be done about this? Probably nothing. It was perhaps inevitable that a utilitarian society would generate a utilitarian environmentalism, and inevitable too that the greens would not be able to last for long outside the established political bunkers. But for me, now – well, this is no longer mine, that's all. I can't make my peace with people who cannibalise the land in the name of saving it. I can't speak the language of science without a corresponding poetry. I can't speak with a straight face about saving the planet when what I really mean is saving myself from what is coming.

Like all of us, I am a foot soldier of empire. It is the empire of *Homo sapiens sapiens* and it stretches from Tasmania to Baffin Island. Like all empires, it is built on expropriation and exploitation, and like all empires it dresses these things up in the language of morality and duty. When we turn wilderness over to agriculture, we speak of our duty to feed the poor. When we industrialise the wild places, we speak of our duty to stop the climate from changing. When we spear whales, we speak of our duty to science. When we raze forests, we speak of our duty to develop. We alter the atmospheric make-up of the entire world: half of us pretends it's not happening, the other half immediately starts looking for new machines that will reverse it. This is how empires work, particularly when they have started to decay. Denial, displacement, anger, fear.

The environment is the victim of this empire. But 'the environment' – that distancing word, that empty concept – does not exist. It is the air, the waters, the creatures we make homeless or lifeless in flocks and legions, and it is us too. We are it; we are in it and of it, we make it and live it, we are fruit and soil and tree, and the things done to the roots and the leaves come back to us. We make ourselves slaves to make ourselves free, and when the shackles start to rub we confidently predict the emergence of new, more comfortable designs.

I don't have any answers, if by answers we mean political systems, better machines, means of engineering some grand shift in consciousness. All I have is a personal conviction built on those feelings, those responses, that goes back to the moors of northern England and the rivers of southern Borneo – that something big is being missed. That we are both hollow men and stuffed men, and that we will keep stuffing ourselves until the food runs out and if outside the dining-room door we have made a wasteland and called it necessity, then at least we will know we were not to blame, because we are never to blame, because we are the humans.

What am I to do with feelings like these? Useless feelings in a world in which everything must be made useful. Sensibilities in a world of utility. Feelings like this provide no 'solutions'. They build no new eco-homes, remove no carbon from the atmosphere. This is head-in-the-clouds stuff, as relevant to our busy, modern lives as the new moon or the date of Lughnasadh. Easy to ignore, easy to dismiss, like the places that inspire the feelings, like the world outside the bubble, like the people who have seen it, if only in brief flashes beyond the ridge of some dark line of hills.

But this is fine; the dismissal, the platitudes, the brusque moving on of the grown-ups. It's all fine. I withdraw, you see. I withdraw from the campaigning and the marching, I withdraw from the arguing and the talked-up necessity and all of the false assumptions. I withdraw from the words. I am leaving. I am going to go out walking.

I am leaving on a pilgrimage to find what I left behind in the jungles and by the cold campfires and in the parts of my head and my heart that I have been skirting around because I have been busy fragmenting the world in order to save it;

busy believing it is mine to save. I am going to listen to the wind and see what it tells me, or whether it tells me anything at all. You see, it turns out that I have more time than I thought. I will follow the songlines and see what they sing to me and maybe, one day, I might even come back. And if I am very lucky I might bring with me a harvest of fresh tales, which I can scatter like apple seeds across this tired and angry land.

Dark Mountain, issue 1, 2010

The Poet and the Machine

or A Tale of Three Thomases

Edward Thomas, the post-Georgian poet, experienced a painfully brief flowering of his creativity – a few years of verse, unnoticed in his lifetime – before he went to the trenches in World War One and was silenced by the guns. His poems are close-up studies of rural south England in its last Golden Age; the days before its identity and meaning were lost for ever, before the war and the car and the suburbs ate it alive.

At hawthorn-time in Wiltshire travelling
In search of something chance would never bring

Travelling before the national grid and the motorways, before the bombing planes and the suburbs and the business parks and the factory shops. At hawthorn time in Wiltshire today the hawthorn can still make you catch your breath, but Thomas's world is long gone. Golden Ages are always just too far back to touch, something that Thomas himself seemed to know. ('The past', he wrote, 'is the only dead thing that smells sweet.')

In his introduction to the painfully slim *Selected Poems*, his namesake, the Welsh poet R. S. Thomas, suggested intriguingly that 'somewhere beyond the borders of Thomas' mind, there was a world he could never quite come at'. That phrase, that image, has always stuck with me. R. S. was referring – as he always referred – to a quasi-mystical Welshness of the blood, which he believed the younger man had been influenced by, and which he offered as a partial explanation for 'the vein of melancholy and dissatisfaction which runs through Edward Thomas' verse'.

Of course there's something very English, too, about melancholy and dissatisfaction, and I'm not at all sure that the Celtic imagination was what Edward Thomas was trying to come at in his writing. I think, rather, that his dissatisfaction, and the almost painfully evocative poems that flowed from it, may have been a result of living in a world on the brink. A coming European war hung over the rural railway stations and hawthorn lanes of which Thomas wrote and, beyond that, the tearing-up of everything he loved in the pre-motor-car and – in many places – still pre-modern English countryside.

> *I never had noticed it until*
> *'Twas gone, – the narrow copse*
> *Where now the woodman lops*
> *The last of the willows with his bill*

Thomas never lived to see what industrial agriculture, mass car ownership or consumer capitalism would do to that countryside, but I think he must have felt, on those lonely walks down the holloways, a foreboding. A function of poetry is to give words to intuitions that, if expressed in prose, would fall apart under their own flimsiness; to see what is coming and try to express it and not to have it understood until everybody else can also see it, at which point they will claim that they saw it all along.

Sometimes I think I might know how Edward Thomas felt. He was in love with the lanes and the downs and the people who called them home, and he knew – no, he intuited, felt but could never quite intellectualise – that these things were flaming down a dying arc. He knew he would love and lose, and he wrote to understand how to live with that. The battlefields of Flanders meant that he never had to.

I used to read Thomas religiously, and would often wonder what state he was in before he was killed in 1917, at Arras, at the same age I am now. How did he feel? What gripped him? The melancholy, still? Despair? Stoicism? Even hope? He had a wife and children back at home. He must have known that, if he ever got back, nothing would ever be the same; that walks down the same lanes could never conjure the same lines.

> *Now I know that Spring will come again,*
> *Perhaps to-morrow: however late I've patience*
> *After this night following on such a day.*

Edward Thomas was in love with a world that was dying, and all he could do was be present. Perhaps this is a timeless human condition, or at least a Western condition (we often confuse the two). The sweep of history is the story of worlds dying, after all. Perhaps it is the poet's condition (the theft of his world literally sent John Clare mad). It's certainly a condition that speaks to us today.

Recently, I have been researching the impact that humanity has had on the natural world since I was born, in 1972. It's been sobering. Since my birth, *Homo sapiens sapiens* has managed to kill off between a quarter and a third of all the world's wild – i.e. non-human – life. This bald figure takes in 25 per cent of all land-based species, 28 per cent of marine species and 29 per cent of freshwater species. We've wiped out 35 per cent of the planet's mangrove swamps and 20 per cent of its coral, over a quarter of all remaining Arctic wildlife and 600,000 square kilometres of Amazon forest. Extinction rates are currently between a hundred and a thousand times higher than they would likely be were humans not around. This is before we even get to climate change. And it has all happened in less than forty years.

Sit back and think about the magnitude of that. Try even to begin to understand its scale and scope and speed. You can't; not really. Beyond a certain point, numbers like these hinder rather than help comprehension. Humans were not built to think on this scale, which may be how we got to this point, and we think primarily in stories, not statistics. But however we got here, our current challenge, it seems to me, is to face this sometimes agonising reality openly and honestly, and without any pill-sugaring fantasy talk of turning it all around with 'sustainability' or UN treaties or revolutions or ethical shopping.

The second Thomas – R. S., the caustic and contradictory Welsh priest whose later poems in particular are bombs thrown into the cosy front rooms of his countryfolk – used to refer to the onward march of industrial civilisation simply as 'the Machine':

> *. . . The still, small voice*
> *is that of Orpheus looking*
> *over his shoulder at a dream*
> *fading. At the mouth*

of the cave is the machine's
whirlwind, hurrying the new
arts in.

Thomas feared and loathed the Machine so much that he used to preach to his rural parishioners, according to his son, about 'the evils of fridges'. His wife tore the central heating out of their ancient Welsh cottage to escape from those new arts which were breathing at her door. But Thomas knew – intuited – that the Machine could not be stopped, only lived with. He lived with it by increasingly retreating into a kind of Celtic Twilight (one brilliantly captured by Byron Rogers's biography of the poet) – moving further and further west, to smaller and smaller parishes, searching for a place to belong and never finding it because the search turned out to be the goal, if ever there was a goal at all.

I am as prone to nostalgia as both Thomases, and visions of past Golden Ages hold a visceral appeal for me. I can dream of those pre-industrial hawthorn lanes for hours, dream until I can physically smell them. But they're gone, like so much else is going, and we are going to have to live with it. Nostalgia is one of life's pleasures, but it can only, in the end, take you down a dead end.

Perhaps the answer is summed up by a third Thomas, Dylan, whose famous injunction to 'Rage, rage against the dying of the light' calls angrily for a last stand even when the battle is clearly lost. That's part of it, I think: a determination to fight for what is good and right, to fight against the encroachments of the Machine even though you know that the Machine does not die, only ever slumbers; takes blows but always rises again, because the Machine is us and part of us loves it even as it takes our world apart.

What does this mean in practice? It means, I think, respecting the past – its tools and technologies, our connection to it, the fact that it continues to live in us – without collapsing into nostalgia for it. It means understanding that nothing is coming back, that the future will be very different from then and now, but that the future will be very different from how we recently understood it to be also. Not only will we not be getting the jetpacks and moon bases I was hoping for as a child; we will not be getting the pensions and secure jobs I was told to work towards as a student. The future looks more like feeling in the dark as our certainties collapse. But it also looks like holding on to whatever we can of the world beyond the human.

Anything could happen in the next hundred years. The two extremes? Well, we could devastate the Earth and collapse into chaos and runaway climate change. Or we could create a global 'sustainable' society based on large-scale renewable tech, mass rollout of GM crops, nanotechnology and geoengineering – a controlled world of controlled people living in a closely monitored scientific monoculture. Brave New World with windfarms and smartphones. Which would be better? Who would deliberately aim for either? Why do both look frighteningly possible?

Faced with these poles, the middle way looks like a stumble towards the guns armed only with penknives and tin trays. But that's where we are. What it means, I think, is that our task – mine, anyway, because I wouldn't want to speak for anyone else – is to save as much of the wild world as can be saved, even if that means buying half an acre of English woodland and starting a coppice cycle to get the butterflies and the birds back. And it is to practise and to teach ways of being and doing that worked once, work now and will work tomorrow, when the cars look as lumbering as airships and the roads have gone from dirt to asphalt and back again.

Something Edward Thomas would still recognise today is *Papaver rhoeas* – the common poppy. Famously, these flowers sprang up all over the battlefields of Flanders where Thomas died. They did so because the common poppy seed can lie dormant in the soil for up to eighty years – it can be paved over, built on or oversown, and it will wait patiently until the plough or the guns tear up the soil again and breathe life into it. The common poppy flowers when everything is turned upside down.

Be a poppy then, in the face of the Machine? It seems a good task to set myself. To watch and learn and save and sow seeds and wait for them to flower, knowing that they may not do so in my lifetime. In an age of loss, our task is surely to keep safe what we can when the Machine passes by, hungry and howling for blood. To be still and stoical and protective, to pass on truths and skills that will always be truths and skills, and never forget to remember what we are losing, every day that we live.

Poems quoted are Edward Thomas's 'Lob', 'First Known When Lost' and 'March', and R. S. Thomas's 'One Life'.

dark-mountain.net, 2011

Learning What to Make of It

When we win, it's with small things, and the triumph itself makes us small. What is extraordinary and eternal does not *want* to be bent by us.

Rainer Maria Rilke

Certain gardens are described as retreats when they are really attacks.

Ian Hamilton Finlay

The most exciting thing in my life at the moment is a five-gallon bucket full of human excrement.

I should explain.

I recently tore the flush toilet out of our family home and replaced it with a compost toilet that I built myself. It is of the most basic variety: we crap into a big bucket and cover the crap with sawdust. When the bucket is full I empty the contents onto a compost heap, where it rots down over the course of a year. At the end of that year, we should have a safe and nutritious compost to use on our fruit trees and bushes, on the fuel coppices of aspen and birch we'll be planting this winter, and on the small native forest that we are planning to grow here for as long as we are healthy.

It's a major job, something like this, and undertaking it has made me realise how much effort needs to be put into the most simple things, and that in turn has made me realise why the society I live in has become addicted to paying for complicated things instead, and how this has laid a great big elephant trap for us that we may struggle ever to get out of. But I'm getting ahead of myself.

The first thing I did was to build a rectangular box out of planks and nails, and the remains of two kitchen cupboard doors, which we didn't need any more. There followed a lot of sanding and planing and painting and varnishing and swearing when things were the wrong length and hinges didn't fit where they should have done. This took a few weeks, on and off, but at the end of it I had quite a handsome varnished wooden structure with two shiny-blue hinged covers and a toilet seat on top. A five-gallon brewing bucket fitted underneath.

Then I had to build a compost heap: two, in fact, so that we could keep an annual cycle of compost from the toilet going. I bought some old pallets from the timber yard up the road and carted them home in my van. That was a couple of days' work. After I had finished, I stood back and admired them for about half an hour. I am a writer. I have never been a practical man, or have never believed I am, and I'm still at the stage where successfully completing a practical task fills me with astonishment.

Still, that was the easy bit. Ever tried taking out a flush toilet? It's a messy job. In the end, a friend came round and devoted an afternoon to helping me to do it. He is a casually practical man, so the job went well. In the aftermath, big chunks of porcelain lay on the grass outside and all that remained in the bathroom was a blocked-up outflow pipe and a gash in the lino. In went the compost loo; in went a bucket of sawdust; in went a wall hanging to cover the gaping holes, and *voilà*: a closed-loop system.

The flush toilet, to me, is a worthy metaphor for the civilisation I live in. It is convenient, it is easy, it is hygienic and it is wonderfully warm and dry. It is the most luxurious pooing experience known to man. You can do your business and never have to think about what happens next: never have to think about what happens to the faeces and urine you have just produced, just as you probably never thought about the origins of the food that created it in the first place. You can act, if you like, as if you have never produced it at all; as if you were far too civilised to have to engage in such base and primitive behaviour. You can sit in the warmth, reading an amusing light-hearted book, then you can simply press a button, and you will never have to deal with your own shit.

What happens to a society that won't deal with its own shit? It ends up deep in it.

A compost toilet is harder work. First you have to build the toilet and the compost heaps, and then you have to source a regular supply of sawdust or pine needles, which will keep the smells and flies away and give the compost enough bulk on the heap. Most importantly, you have to empty the bucket when it gets full, which is every few days most of the time. This is the part of the job that really seems to disgust those of my friends and family who can't understand why I have disposed of a perfectly good toilet and replaced it with something medieval.

But it's also the part of the job that I enjoy the most. I've noticed myself getting almost excited as the bucket approaches being full. Emptying the thing onto the compost heap, covering it with grass, inspecting the progress of the heap so far, cleaning and replacing the bucket, putting a new layer of sawdust in the bottom: would you believe me if I told you this was a satisfying process? Anticipating being able to use the results on my own trees is almost thrilling.

If a flush toilet is a metaphor for a civilisation that wants to wash its hands of its own wastes as long as they accumulate somewhere else, then a compost toilet is both a small restitution, and a declaration: I will not turn my back on the consequences of my actions. I will not hand them over to someone else to deal with. I will not crap into clean drinking water and flush it down a pipe to be cleaned with industrial chemicals at some sewage plant I have never visited. I will fertilise my own ground with my own manure, and in doing so I will control an important part of my life in this world, and that control will give me more understanding over it. I will claw something of myself back. Even in the rain, even in winter, I will deal with my own shit.

*

In 2014, I emigrated. My wife and I moved with our two young children from urban England, where we had always lived, to rural Ireland. We bought ourselves a small bungalow with two and a half acres of land up a quiet lane. It was the culmination of a personal project we've been engaged in for more than half a decade: to find a way to escape from the urban consumer machine we were both brought up in.

We wanted to live more simply; or perhaps just more starkly, because life here is rarely simple. Our kids were just getting to school age, and the idea of sending them to school to systematically crush their spontaneity and have them taught computer coding so that they could compete in the 'global race' made us miserable. We wanted to grow our own food and compost our own shit and educate our own children and make our own jam and take responsibility for our own actions.

This can all sound very cloying. Western middle-class people going 'back to the land' is a modern cliché, and when we think we are hearing that story we tend to react in a particular way, positive or negative depending on our political or cultural persuasions. Perhaps I am a cliché, but I'm not especially interested in other people's expectations. I was brought here by many things, but one of them is a voice that has been whispering in my ear for years, and growing louder for the last few.

This voice tells me that I am one of the luckiest people on Earth. It tells me I am a middle-class man from a country grown fat on centuries of plunder, that I have a university degree, that I go to restaurants and have a laptop computer and an internet connection, and I can publish articles like this in magazines. In other words, I am somewhere up near the top of the pyramid of human material fortune. And that in turn means I am up near the top of the pyramid of human cupidity and destruction that is driving the natural world to the edge.

One of the driving forces in my life is a deep love of nature. If you ask me to explain precisely what I mean by that, or why it has such a grip on me, I won't be able to. But I could tell you about profound experiences I've had in forests and mountains, about the joy that rises in my heart when I see a hawk circle or hear the roar of an untamed river, and the misery that sinks into it if I'm trapped in a city or on a motorway. I could tell you about the occasional brief glimpses I get into the reality that I am a passing moment in an ancient, beautiful, terrifying whorl of life on a vast unknowable planet; that I am not an observer of it, but a part of its wide flow; that there is no such thing as outside. This kind of thing is nearly impossible to put down on paper, as you can see. Once upon a time, many millennia ago, I suspect it would have been the default worldview, but today, it is a hard one to live with. The culture that I was born into is systematically dismantling the web of life itself, and as it does so it is dismantling my sense of meaning and many of the things that I love. My status as a middle-class consumer in a Western industrialised country means that I am part of this problem, whether I want to face up to that or not.

This is what that voice whispered to me, as once it whispered to Rilke: *you must change your life.* I came here because I can't justify my complicity any more. I feel a personal duty to live as simply and with as little impact on the rest of nature as I possibly can. I've no interest in extending this duty to anybody else, or in preaching about it or politicising it, or in pretending that I am in any way pure or unsullied or even halfway competent yet at undertaking it. It is just a personal calling.

But perhaps it explains my joy at that full toilet bucket. I feel I am at last starting to do my bit, to make restitution, to walk the walk after so many years of talking the talk. I can't write or talk about natural beauty, or natural anything, unless I'm trying to do as little damage to it as possible; and at this time in history, that means taking myself away from the heart of the beast. It means stripping back. It means inconveniencing myself. It means paying attention.

*

Soon after I got here I began reading a new collection of letters between the poet-activists Wendell Berry and Gary Snyder,* both of them influences on my own writing, both role models in some ways. They jumped ship and bought themselves acres of land many decades ago, and they stuck it out. And here they were, discussing the nature of modernity, the problem of technology, the life of the spirit and how to use a chainsaw, in handwritten letters over a period of forty years. It was the right book at the right time.

In July 1973, Berry wrote to Snyder with some important news. He had bought forty acres of land in his native Kentucky, to add to the twelve acres he already owned. This made him the owner and manager of a fifty-two-acre farm: a steward of the land as his Kentucky ancestors had been. 'All this adds up to a profound event,' writes Berry. 'We'll be years, I think, learning what to make of it.'

My two and a half acres seem profound enough to a boy from the suburbs who has never even owned a garden. At the time of writing, we've been here seven months. It took about three months for it to stop feeling like a holiday, though the children settled in more quickly than their parents did, building dens in the bushes and making a home in a fairy tree at the edge of the field. Children adapt to any-

---

* *Distant Neighbors: The Selected Letters of Wendell Berry and Gary Snyder*, Counterpoint Press, 2014.

thing if they haven't been told what normal is. And just in the last few weeks, I've felt myself beginning to settle too; to sink into the place a little.

I've noticed the different birds that appear around the house in the different seasons: the bullfinches in April, the swallows in June, the starlings in October, the robins and wrens at Christmas. I've noticed myself not wanting so much, and not wanting to leave. Even buying a few items of food every week seems an indulgence. Making things from stuff we find lying about feels like an act of resistance or escape: compost heaps from old bits of wood, firewood from fallen trees, cordial from blackberries, water butts from old barrels. We use less water; we produce less rubbish. Sometimes I feel small spaces open up in my life where anxiety used to be. Only sometimes, and briefly. Still, it feels like something is being reawakened.

In 2009, I was one of the founders of an initiative called the Dark Mountain Project. It began life as a self-published manifesto written by me and another writer, and it grew out of a need to find new ways of relating to the struggle over the future of nature in a human-centred world. Having spent years as an environmentalist working to 'save the world', I no longer believed that any such thing was possible. I thought that climate change was going to tip us over the brink much sooner than we thought, and that most people alive today, if given the choice between the kind of comfortable lifestyle I spend too much time agonising about, and the sacrifices needed to prevent the ecocide we are unleashing across the globe, would choose the former.

I thought then, and still think, that the momentum of the global civilisation we have built is unstoppable, and that its conclusion will be either its own collapse, the destruction of most life on Earth or the refashioning of Earth entirely in the image and interests of modern human beings. Either way, the oil tanker is not turning around now, despite the heroic efforts of many. 'The best intentions in the world', wrote Snyder to Berry, 'will not stop the inertia of a heavy civilisation that is rolling on its way.' That was in 1977. I was five.

Wondering where that left me was the starting point for the Dark Mountain Project, which has since evolved into a network of writers, artists, thinkers and doers across the world. Dark Mountain began as an attempt to found, or discover, a new form of literature: one more engaged with, and honest about, the age of ecocide we find ourselves in. It is still that, but it is something else too: something it was never intended to be but that, in retrospect, it had to be. It is a way to work through the grief caused by the end of much of what we hold dear.

Living through the Earth's sixth mass extinction, and knowing that our species is the cause of it, can be similar in some ways to living through the death of a loved one, or the collapse of something important and precious in your life. Before you can move on, before you can accept what has happened and come to terms with it, you need to be able to grieve, in the company of others. You need to be able to acknowledge the reality of the loss, and the pain it causes. You need to stop pretending that the loss isn't real, or that it will all go back to how it was. Grieving is the starting point for being able to move on and through, and to begin to rebuild yourself again.

In retrospect, this Dark Mountain of ours has offered a way to engage in a kind of planetary grieving process. It has allowed people to come together to talk about the despair they feel at the state of the world and their inability to change what they would like to change. But this is a starting point, not an ending. Accepting the loss and moving through it, dropping old assumptions and thinking afresh, allows you to think again about the big question: how can I still be useful?

For me, the answer to that question has been at least partly discovered in this place. After years of living in cities with barely any contact with the ground, fuelled by anger and righteousness, driving myself into the ground, I decided to exchange activism for action. I decided to dig in, to use my limited powers to improve at least one small square of Earth, and to write, sometimes, about what I discovered by doing so.

Not everyone has been impressed with this approach. Some environmental activists in particular have reacted with anger. All this talk of grief and acceptance has sounded to them like a dangerous abdication of responsibility. It's all very well for you to run away from the 'fight', I have been told, but this is the fate of the Earth we're talking about. Forests are falling; the climate is changing. Millions of people are going to die, and you are advocating doing nothing. Are you depressed? Are you burned out? Whatever is wrong with you, you need to stop talking, because you are getting in the way of the necessary work.

My first reaction to responses like these was to defend myself, but when I got past that, I found I could easily understand their perspective. But I still thought there was something missing. Only two ways of reacting to the current crisis of nature were offered. On the one hand, there was 'fighting'. This fighting was to be aimed at the 'elite' that was destroying the planet – oil companies, politicians, corporate leaders, the rich. On the other hand, there was 'giving up'. Giving up meant not fighting. It meant running away from a necessary battle. It meant being selfish. It meant 'doing nothing', and letting the planet go to hell.

All of this hinged on a narrow definition of what *doing something* involved, and what *action* meant. It seemed to suggest that *action* must be something grand and global and gestural. Small actions were not actions at all: if you couldn't 'change the world' there seemed little point in changing anything. Being seen to be able to say you were 'fighting' rather than 'giving up' could sometimes appear to be more important than whether that fight had any measurable impact. This military language, this focus on action-at-all-costs, this shaming of those who question it, seems strange to me. In an age in which 'fighting for the planet' most often means tweeting, signing petitions, writing blogs and sometimes going on a march, the rhetoric seems not only overblown but likely to obscure the value of more focused, small-scale personal commitments to changing things for the better.

In 1978, Berry wrote to Snyder with a sense of disappointment. He had hoped that by taking on his farm and learning to run it, by engaging with the dirt beneath his feet, he would perhaps be able to step back from his concerns about the state of the wider world. It hadn't worked. 'I see with considerable sorrow', he wrote, 'that I am not going to get done fighting and live at peace in anything like the simple way I once thought I would. So how to keep from becoming evil? Maybe the answer is to fight always *for* what you particularly love, not for abstractions and not *against* anything: don't fight against even the devil, and don't fight to "save the world".'

Berry was getting at something here that seems more significant to me as the years roll by. Traditional leftist 'activism' entrenches a kind of dependency. It involves identifying an enemy and then taking it on. Whether you are fighting or petitioning, there is always a Them who needs to sort out the problem, and that gives Us, the disempowered but righteous masses, more of an excuse to wash our hands of our own complicity, or simply to never get them dirty in the first place.

I don't say any of this to dismiss the value of activism, though I know it can sound like it. My point is not that political organising never works, but that it works only sometimes. When it does work, it is a useful tool. There are elites to be opposed and politicians to be held to account and planting vegetables is not the answer to everything. But nothing is the answer to everything – that's the point. Once you start thinking you are responsible for, or can influence, everything, you are lost. When you take responsibility for a specific something, on the other hand, it's possible you might get somewhere.

I think now that there is a difference between action and activism. I walked away from global environmental politics because its message didn't ring true and because even many of those who were putting it out didn't really seem to believe it. I walked away because I was disillusioned, and because I was getting older, and because I probably was burned out; but also because that kind of activism seemed to be a block on actual, real action. I felt too complicit to keep blaming other people. If I was going to blame anyone, I would rather blame myself. I'm good at that.

*

In 1966, the Scottish artist Ian Hamilton Finlay bought a derelict farm in the Pentland Hills, which he spent decades transforming into a sculpture and poetry garden he named Little Sparta. For years, he barely left the place. But when friends suggested that he had simply built himself a retreat in which to hide from reality, Finlay put them straight. 'Certain gardens', he replied, 'are described as retreats when they are really attacks.'

What did he mean? Perhaps that the beauty and meaning he was constructing around him was an attack on the kind of world that thinks it is meaningless to do something so small, so local, so specific. To tend a garden, to learn to be humble, to use your skills locally rather than globally: none of this will 'save the world', none of it is easy to rally large groups of people behind, none of it makes a good slogan. And yet, it has an impact. Finlay said that one of the things he learned by building his garden was simply that 'you can change a bit of the actual world by taking out a spade of earth'.

We live in a culture that idolises 'big-picture thinking' and dismisses small-picture anything; that puts a premium on action and belittles contemplation. Even those of us who would like to see a very different world from the one we are living in often help to perpetuate its values with our habitual rushing around and our insistence on change over stillness. We are the people of the West, and we believe that the world must be gripped and turned to a shape. Sometimes I think that 'saving the world' is just another way of controlling it.

I see this every day in my own life. I'm writing this essay in a hut at the top of our field. It is a small field, about an acre and a half, hemmed by blackthorn and maple and oak trees, which runs flat for half its length and then rolls down towards an old boreen. The previous owners had cows in it, but with the animals gone it has been running riot. Dock and creeping buttercup have sprouted everywhere, and everything has grown faster than I would have imagined possible. Until I moved here I hadn't known that a bramble creeper can grow by a foot a day. Or at any rate, it seems like it.

In reaction to this, my first instinct was to panic and my second was to take control. Something had to be done! The place was a mess. We had to decide what we were going to do with this field and then do it, quickly, before it became unmanageable. In other words, we needed to grip and dominate the field, shape it to our use, even though we didn't know what that use was because we haven't yet decided what to actually do with it.

Slowly, very slowly, I am learning to relax about this. I am learning that it doesn't matter if I don't know what to do and I am learning, more significantly, that the field itself is not simply a canvas on which I can impose my designs, but a living thing with which I need to negotiate a relationship. Until I see what it is doing, what is growing where, where the wet parts are, where the frost gathers in winter, what trees are in the hedges and what birds are feeding from them, I can't make any useful decisions about anything.

Until I slow down and pay attention, I am more likely to do damage than anything else, and I am more likely to create unnecessary work for myself.

So, recently, I had an idea. I would walk the boundaries of this field once a day for a year, and I would write down what I saw. By the end of the year, I would understand the land better. I would force myself to pay attention: something I'm not instinctively good at doing. I would tear myself out of my head and put myself into this place. I would slow down.

These days, when I feel like mounting an attack, these few green acres seem like the best place to plant my weapons. Because coming here is an attack on myself as well. It is a challenge I issue to the part of me that likes to build abstractions or theories designed to pin the world down, and is tempted to issue rallying cries and sketch out easy answers. It says: here is the mess and the complexity and the hard work. Never mind your concepts. Do you know how to use a mattock?

Of course, I would be lying if I pretended that coming here wasn't also a retreat: it is. It is a retreat from the noise and the stink of the cities, from people with their heads buried in their iPhones. It is a retreat from the tech-soaked iniquities of the modern school system, a retreat from all the marketing bullshit that is thrown at me as I walk down any urban street any day of the week. It is a retreat to a place where I can make myself known, and that I can begin to know. A place where I can gather sloes from the hedges and make them into gin and stack the bottles on top of my fridge and watch them turn slowly crimson over months. Where I can stand on my porch, as I did last night, chopping seasoned beech logs into kindling and watching the sky grow pink in the west. Where I can take a walk down the lane with my small daughter, and on the way back I can watch her climb a farm gate to pick wild plums from a roadside tree, and run home with her pockets full. I doubt I had even seen a wild plum at her age. I call that an education.

This is what I came here for, and in these small moments I remember that. Yes, it is a retreat. But it is not *just* a retreat. I have more work to do than ever; it is just a different kind of work. I've thought for years that the best way to put a spanner in the consumer dystopia that is unfolding is to ground yourself in a place and to learn to do things with your hands – actually learn to do them, not just write about learning to do them. Grow your own carrots, learn to use an axe and a scythe, know where the sun falls and what the trees do and what is growing in the laneways. Get to know your neighbours, put down roots and stay even when you don't want to stay. Be famous, as Gary Snyder so wonderfully suggested, for fifteen miles.

So I'm trying to tune myself into where I am. I'm trying to force myself to slow down and listen. It doesn't come naturally, but when I do it, I feel my perspective subtly shift. I notice the different sounds made by red-tailed and white-tailed bumblebees, or the cackling of the rook on the chimney pot in the morning, or the different times the hawthorn and the blackthorn flower. Most of what lives on this land never notices me. I am learning what to make of it, slowly and clumsily and often impatiently, and it is work that I will never get enough of, and I will never master. Nothing can be done, I think now, except what can be done. Whenever I leave this place, and however, I'd like it to be richer than it was when I found it.

'Do you think it could be a general rule', Berry asked Snyder towards the end of 1979, 'that the only place one is urgently needed is at home?' I think it could be. I think it is.

2014

The Barcode Moment

It was in religious education classes at school that I was first introduced to Satanic Barcode Theory. If you've no idea what I'm talking about, let me explain to you how it works. First, take a quote from the Book of Revelation:

And he ['the Beast'] causeth all, both small and great, rich and poor, free and bond, to receive a mark in their right hand, or in their foreheads: And that no man might buy or sell, save he that had the mark, or the name of the beast, or the number of his name. Here is wisdom. Let him that hath understanding count the number of the beast: for it is the number of a man; and his number is six hundred threescore and six.

That's the Bible, informing you that a time will come when no one will be able to 'buy or sell' without the 'mark of the Beast' on his or her head or hand. That number is 666.

Next, take a look at a barcode: any barcode, on any consumer product. Every barcode, you will notice, is a long array of lines of differing widths. Each of these lines represents a number. When the barcode is scanned, the scanner picks up the unique number it represents and transforms this into a price. But while each barcode is different, all have three identical 'guard bars' at the beginning, the middle and the end. Take a look at your nearest barcode and you'll see them: three bars that are longer than all the others. Each of these guard bars is the equivalent of the number 6.

Every barcode in the world, in other words, has the number 666 running through it like words through a stick of rock. So, the barcode, without which it is pretty tough these days to 'buy or sell' anything, is the mark of the Beast, according to the Bible and my old RE teacher. Satan is capitalism. It's not an unconvincing suggestion.

There are a few flaws in this theory, of course, not least of which is that no one has barcodes tattooed on their head or hand. Yet. But this, I was told, was a detail; my teacher was pretty convinced that, within a few decades, some version of the barcode would end up embedded in or imprinted on human bodies, to allow us all to transact our lives away with minimal fuss.

When I was fifteen, this conspiracy theory was exciting. I wasn't religious, and wasn't in the habit of listening much to RE teachers, but this suggestion grabbed me. It satisfied the Manichaean part of my nature. The world was, in this telling, a straight battle between good and evil, and once people started tattooing barcodes on their skin it was going to be pretty damn clear which was which. At that point, those of us who were good would be able to see what was coming, and we would cut loose: run to the hills, form communes, get guns, prepare. It would be frightening, but also thrilling – and, most importantly of all, morally simple. There was no complexity. You had the mark, or you didn't. And when the moment came, I'd never let them mark me.

You're quite susceptible to this kind of worldview when you're fifteen, you've read *The Lord of the Rings* twice and you watch *Star Wars* every Christmas. Then you grow up and you realise, with some regret, that life is more morally complex than this. You realise that the barcode moment – the moment when the grey areas fall away and you are forced to choose, and you can take your stand with clarity – will never come.

And then you hear about Google Glass.

Google Glass, pioneered by the increasingly frightening Google corporation (whose own company motto, ironically, is 'don't be evil') is a pair of slightly dorky-looking spectacles that stream the internet directly into your eyes, providing you, literally, with a new lens through which to see the world: one manufactured by a big and exceptionally ambitious corporation. One that defines and explains that world to you, mediated by corporate algorithms moulded to your own specific consumer preferences, which will doubtless make every effort to sell bits of it to you as well. As a breathless review of this infant technology in a geek magazine explains:

> The Google goggles can give weather information when you look out the window, show you a text message and allow you to reply with voice dictation and more. One section of the video shows the glasses informing the user that the underground system is suspended before they enter the station and goes on to give turn-by-turn walking directions to the destination . . . We don't know how far away from getting hold of a pair of these we are but we hope it's sooner rather than later.

Google, naturally, has been regaling us with possibilities. Wearing these, you'll be able to look at a tree and be informed what species it is; look at a cloud and get a flashing message in the sky giving you its meteorological name; look at a product and get a price. The whole world will be labelled and tagged. You'll be an excited, well-informed robot-person, all day every day, and there'll be no need at all for even minimal interaction with your surroundings or with other living creatures.

I'm not qualified to say whether Google is the Antichrist, though nothing would surprise me any more. Perhaps my old RE teacher would know. But I think that, if this technology ever becomes a widespread reality, this could be my barcode moment. This could be the point at which I run for the hills. Because this crosses some ill-defined but strongly felt internal line. This is the point at which technologies that up to now have merely been irritating and sometimes a bit worrying – smartphones, mobile Twitter feeds, handheld devices and the like – become actually sinister. This is the point at which our dive head first into human narcissism – our declaration that we will not interact any more with anything but ourselves and our machines – becomes stark and impossible to deny.

But what would I be running from, and how could I escape it? This is the future. It is the direction this culture is headed in. It is the rational next step in a progressive narrative that sees us escaping from nature and merging with – becoming – machines. It is the remaking of everything in the image of the hive mind of the consumer West.

'Give a Western man a job of work to do', wrote George Orwell eighty years ago, 'and he will immediately set about inventing a machine to do it for him.' Today perhaps we could update this rule for the digital age: give a Western man a choice between engaging with his internal world through a machine or engaging with the external world via his body and its immediate environment, and he'll increasingly choose the former. Perhaps it's only a small step from the chip in your smartphone to the chip in your head or your hand. I'm not sure I'd count anything out. But certainly the endpoint of a culture that focuses on human desire above all things, rejects all previous ways of living, worships machines, sneers at the spiritual and sees the world as a collection of components to be taken apart and analysed in the service of utility, is a world in which humanity disappears further and further into narcissistic virtuality, 'improving' its own capabilities with its technology while the world burns around it.

Or is it? Is there even an 'endpoint' at all? Perhaps this is the wrong way to look at what is happening here. Because we are not faced with that Manichaean choice I once imagined we would come to: are you man or machine? We find ourselves, instead, on a spectrum; or perhaps on a slow train, with a clear direction of travel but with no defined stops. Where – whether – to jump off? It is never clear.

Google Glass might provide my barcode moment, but everyone has to choose their own, if they have one. At what point will you jump from the train – and where will you land? At what point will the merger between humans and their machines frighten or disgust you so much that the wake-up call becomes too loud to ignore? I know people for whom the advent of email and the internet provided that moment. Someone I respect recently described the internet simply as 'a trap', and it was hard to disagree, though it didn't stop me using it.

We are already merging with our technologies. I have sat in pubs with people who play with their smartphones rather than talk to me (perhaps it's just me) and walked down country lanes with people who are too busy Tweeting to notice the tweeting. Twenty years ago this stuff would have been unthinkable. In twenty years' time it will look primitive.

But how far back should we go to trace the beginning of this merger? What would a hunter-gatherer from the Mesolithic think if she were somehow able to travel here and examine a twenty-first-century human? If she were to look at me, with a plastic and steel contraption on my eyes to enhance my vision, and metal in my teeth and an old scar inside my throat where my tonsils were surgically removed and, who knows, in twenty-five years' time a silicon artificial hip and a couple of new heart valves made out of parts of a pig? Would she not think that she had seen the post-human future?

Or does this trajectory go back to the creation of language itself? Or of writing – a form of symbolism that allows us to overlay our intellectual abstractions onto messy reality? Here you are, reading my words; here I am, trying to communicate with you. Is this not a deeply weird way of interacting? We are not responding to each others' body language, or smiles or frowns. There is no chit-chat, no animal relationship at work, no drawing on the ancient intuitions of our species that allow us to converse person to person, with all that this entails. You have probably never even met me. There is just this monologue, cast in lines on a page. We may stimulate each others' brains, but the rest of us sits inert, gazing in on the symbols. The novelist William

Golding – a Christian, though an idiosyncratic one – believed that the biblical Fall came with the development of language. At that point, we had moved inexorably towards abstraction and away from reality, and our fate was sealed.

Perhaps this is really a question of what we get used to and how quickly we get used to it, and how we assume that our small, personal experiences represent something static and unchanging, though this is almost never the case. Grow up with books, as I did, and books seem normal. How would they have seemed to someone from an oral culture? Alien? Inhuman? Perhaps.

When I think about this I think, strangely, about my childhood. I grew up in Middlesex; or rather, that part of greater London which was once Middlesex. My Middlesex was an endless suburb. The local park and the drain under the tube line we played in, the always-closed cricket pavilion, the junior school with the asphalt playground and the blackberries in the hedges. The old toyshop on the bridge, the garages behind the council estate, the thin strips of back garden, the fake-beamed Ind Coope pub from which emanated the exciting and glamorous smell of stale bitter. This was the Middlesex of my childhood. These are my blue remembered hills.

But there were once other Middlesexes, that I am much too young to have seen. This place had been, before the arrival of the Romans, a great forest of oak, elm and beech, inhabited by elk, wolf and deer. Later, the home of the Middle-Saxons became the second-smallest county in England, a retreat for merchants from the noise and grime of London. It developed into an agricultural 'home county' with a distinct character – small, hidden, human-scale –

which made its loss the harder to take for those who knew it. These days, Middlesex barely exists. It has all been swallowed up by London, and even those who live there don't use the county's name any more. There is only a memory where a place used to be.

I discovered John Betjeman, the chronicler of the death of Middlesex, in my early twenties. I discovered old-fashioned poems about places I knew – Harrow, Greenford, Rayner's Lane, Ruislip – in guises that meant nothing to me. It was like seeing a picture of your mother at eighteen, young and free and with no idea you will ever be born. Here was a county of whispering pines, enormous hayfields, elm trees, meadowlands, low, laburnum-leaned-on railings. The evocation of its loss was strong and clean and managed to raise a nostalgia in me for something I had never been part of.

For it wasn't the world I knew. I knew pavements and park railings and cul-de-sacs and council estates and concrete street lamps and white dogshit and the remains of old air-raid sirens. Compared to its past richness, my Middlesex was a drab monoculture. It was, in Betjeman's words, 'silent under soot and stone'. But I liked it, because it was where I came from.

I wonder now whether we could Middlesex the whole world. I wonder if we could replace the rainforests with plantations, fish out the seas until only a couple of commercial species are left, carpet the moors in turbines and dam all the rivers and build endless suburbs over what remains of the hay meadows that are now used to grow maize for silage. I wonder if we could busy ourselves with our microchips and machines, turning the world into a planetary farm to support our digital appetites and sinking deeper into our machine-led narcissism as we do. I wonder if we could deplete the diversity and richness of this wild world by 80 or 90 per cent – and within a few generations see it all forgotten, even by those who noticed its going. I wonder if, raised in this culture, with all the new toys to play with, wearing our Google Glasses, sitting in our self-driving cars, we would even notice, or care?

Our current plunge into ecological overshoot could lead to global economic collapse. Our pushing up against ecological limits could lead to the unplanned scaling back of the human machine. The planet itself may rebel. That's the fear – or the hope, depending on your point of view. But what if the fear is wrong? What if we somehow manage to get ourselves out of this fix? What if the Silicon Valley cornutopians are right, and technology or ingenuity or blind luck save us? Or what if Earth reacts differently; what if it can, after all, tolerate the elimination of 80 per cent of terrestrial life? What if a planet of rats, cockroaches, pigeons, GM crops, synthetic livestock and post-human immortals is possible after all?

In other words, what if this ongoing fear of 'collapse', which I seem so often to come back to in my writing, is a narrative designed to quell a worse fear: that things might not collapse, but continue like this? That the Earth's final wild frontiers may be tamed and diluted, ravaged and destroyed, and that we would not care much because we were too busy following the logic of our narrative to its endpoint, becoming our machines – our little creations, made in our own image, sent out to rule the world with our culture's poison in their silicon veins?

The professional 'futurist' Steve Fuller, author of the predictably titled book *Humanity 2.0*, insists that our direction of travel is now set: that a merger with our machines is not only inevitable but will be popular and beneficial. 'People are voting with their feet to enter Humanity 2.0 with the time they spend in front of computers, as opposed to having direct contact with physical human beings,' he chunters blithely. 'In all this, it's not so much that we've been losing our humanity but that it's becoming projected or distributed across things that lack a human body. In any case, Humanity 2.0 is less about the power of new technologies than a state of mind in which we see our lives fulfilled in such things.'

I suspect he's probably right, and I think that many people, given the opportunity, will want this to go further without much thinking about the implications. But for those of us who don't – those of us who think we can identify a point beyond which we are not personally prepared to plunge into this – what then? What do we do? How do we live?

This question is not new either. Seek out Samuel Butler's 1872 novel *Erewhon*: it is about a society whose members choose to destroy all technology created after a particular date, precisely because they have realised that the endpoint of technological progress would be the end of humanity as they know it. I've already mentioned George Orwell, who speculates at length in *The Road to Wigan Pier* on 'the tendency of the machine to make a fully human life impossible', and how the inevitable endpoint of this vision of progress is the human being reduced to 'a brain in a bottle'. If and when we choose to revolt personally against this, we are revolting not against something new in itself, but simply to the next step on a very old journey away from external nature and towards an internal world in which we get to create our own exclusively human version of reality.

It is more than likely that any rebels against this vision will be in the minority. But so what? If you treat this not as a 'global issue', which requires some kind of mass political response, but instead as a personal experience you have to live through, things start to look rather different. I usually find that the small picture is the most important one. You can think about 'global issues' until your head hurts and you want to die of despair: it is another form of abstraction. We live by the small things: the things we can control or experience personally.

There are fewer and fewer things, in a consumer economy, that we are encouraged or permitted to control. But if we want to, we are still free to make different lives for ourselves to whatever degree we can manage it. We are as free (for now) to say no to Google Glass as we are to say no to credit cards or cars or supermarket shopping. That doesn't mean escaping from the machine – that's impossible – but it means negotiating a relationship with it that gives us as much autonomy as we need or can get or can cope with. In these times, this is probably the best we're ever going to do.

Personally, I have always been with Orwell and with D. H. Lawrence: the techno-industrial culture dehumanises us, sucks out of us some animal essence, which it is impossible perhaps to explain but can be clearly intuited by those who are paying attention. But we can't react to this by trying to globalise or politicise these intuitions. We don't have to be 'activists', campaigning to try and make our particular view of virtual technology the dominant one. This kind of approach is doomed to fail and will likely lead to despair, just as the attempt to prevent climate change and environmental crisis in this way is leading to despair. There are tides in the affairs of men, and standing on the beach ordering the waves back does not make you brave or forward-thinking.

This is a personal view of course, and one I have been developing for a long time, but it seems to me that a kind of strategic retreat is both the best way to ensure personal sanity and to keep the flame of a particular, pre-machine vision of humanity alive. We all choose our own personal visions. I have written about retreating and withdrawing several times before, and it has often brought down on my head accusations of 'defeatism' and the like from the activist-minded. But it's not about defeat, or surrender. It's about pulling back to a place where you can find the breathing space to be free and human again. From that, all else follows, if you can pay attention.

dark-mountain.net, 2012

Dark Ecology

Take the only tree that's left,
Stuff it up the hole in your culture.
Leonard Cohen, 'The Future'

Retreat to the desert, and fight!
D. H. Lawrence

The handle, which varies in length according to the height of its user, and in some cases is made by that user to his or her specifications, is like most of the other parts of the tool in that it has a name and thus a character of its own. I call it the snath, as do most of us in this country, though variations include the snathe, the snaithe, the snead and the sned. Onto the snath are attached two hand grips, adjusted for the height of the user. On the bottom of the snath is a small hole, a rubberised protector and a metal D-ring with two hex sockets. Into this little assemblage slides the tang of the blade.

This thin crescent of steel is the fulcrum of the whole tool. From the genus *blade* fans out a number of ever-evolving species, each seeking out and colonising new niches. My collection includes a number of grass blades of varying styles – a Luxor, a Profisense, several Austrians and a new, elegant Concari Felice blade that I've not even tried yet – whose lengths vary between 60 and 85 centimetres. I also have a couple of ditch blades (which despite the name are not used for mowing ditches particularly, but are all-purpose cutting tools that can manage anything from fine grass to tousled brambles) and a bush blade, which is as thick as a billhook and can take down small trees. These are the big mammals you can see and hear. Beneath and around them scuttle any number of harder-to-spot competitors for the summer grass, all finding their place in the ecosystem of the tool.

None of them, of course, are any use at all unless they are kept sharp, really sharp: sharp enough that if you were to run your finger lightly along the edge you would lose blood. You need to take a couple of stones out into the field with you and use them regularly – every five minutes or so – to keep the edge honed. And you need to know how to use your peening anvil, and when. *Peen* is a word of Scandinavian origin, originally meaning 'to beat iron thin with a hammer', which is still its meaning, though the iron has now been replaced by steel. When the edge of your blade thickens with over-use and over-sharpening, you need to draw the edge out by peening it – cold-forging the blade with hammer and small anvil. It's a tricky job. I've been doing it for years but I've still not mastered it. Probably you never master it, just as you never really master anything. That lack of mastery, and the promise of one day reaching it, is part of the complex beauty of the tool.

Etymology can be interesting. *Scythe*, originally rendered *sithe*, is an Old English word, indicating that the tool has been in use in these islands for at least a thousand years. But archaeology pushes that date much further out; Roman scythes have been found with blades nearly two metres long. Basic, curved cutting tools for use on grass date back at least ten thousand years, to the dawn of agriculture and thus to the dawn of civilisations. Like the tool, the word, too, has older origins. The Proto-Indo-European root of *scythe* is the word *sek*, meaning to cut, or to divide. *Sek* is also the root word of sickle, saw, schism, sex and science.

*

I've recently begun reading the collected writings of Theodore Kaczynski. I'm worried that it may change my life. Some books do that, from time to time, and this is beginning to shape up as one of them.

It's not that Kaczynski, who is a fierce, uncompromising critic of the techno-industrial system, is saying anything I haven't heard before. I've heard it all before, many times. By his own admission, his arguments are not new. But the clarity with which he makes them, and his refusal to obfuscate, are refreshing. I seem to be at a point in my life where I am open to hearing this again. I don't know quite why.

Here are the four premises with which he begins the book:

1. Technological progress is carrying us to inevitable disaster;
2. Only the collapse of modern technological civilisation can avert disaster;
3. The political left is technological society's first line of defence against revolution;
4. What is needed is a new revolutionary movement, dedicated to the elimination of technological society.

Kaczynski's prose is sparse, and his arguments logical and unsentimental, as you might expect from a former mathematics professor with a degree from Harvard. I have a tendency towards sentimentality around these issues, so I appreciate his discipline. I'm about a third of the way through the book at the moment, and the way that the four arguments are being filled out is worryingly convincing. Maybe it's what scientists call 'confirmation bias', but I'm finding it hard to muster good counter-arguments to any of them, even the last. I say 'worryingly' because I do not want to end up agreeing with Kaczynski. There are two reasons for this.

Firstly, if I do end up agreeing with him – and with other such critics I have been exploring recently, such as Jacques Ellul and D. H. Lawrence and C. S. Lewis and Ivan Illich – I am going to have to change my life in quite profound ways. Not just in the ways I've already changed it (getting rid of my telly, not owning a credit card, avoiding smartphones and e-readers and satnavs, growing at least some of my own food, learning practical skills, fleeing the city, etc.) but properly, deeply. I am still embedded, at least partly because I can't work out where to jump, or what to land on, or whether you can ever get away by jumping, or simply because I'm frightened to close my eyes and walk over the edge.

I'm writing this on a laptop computer, by the way. It has a broadband connection and all sorts of fancy capabilities I have never tried or wanted to use. I mainly use it for typing. You might think this makes me a hypocrite, and you might be right, but there is a more interesting observation you could make. This, says Kaczynski, is where we all find ourselves, until and unless we choose to break out. In his own case, he explains, he had to go through a personal psychological collapse as a young man before he could escape what he saw as his chains. He explained this to an interviewer in 2001:

> I knew what I wanted: to go and live in some wild place. But I didn't know how to do so ... I did not know even one person who would have understood why I wanted to do such a thing. So, deep in my heart, I felt convinced that I would never be able to escape from civilisation. Because I found modern life utterly unacceptable, I grew increasingly hopeless until, at the age of 24, I arrived at a kind of crisis: I felt so miserable that I didn't care whether I lived or died. But when I reached that point a sudden change took place: I realised that if I didn't care whether I lived or died, then I didn't need to fear the consequences of anything I might do. Therefore I could do anything I wanted. I was free!

At the beginning of the 1970s, Kaczynski moved to a small cabin in the woods of Montana where he worked to live a self-sufficient life without electricity, hunting and fishing and growing his own food. He lived that way for twenty-five years, trying, initially at least, to escape from civilisation. But it didn't take him long to learn that such an escape, if it was ever possible, is not possible now. More cabins were built in his woods, roads were enlarged, loggers buzzed through his forests. More planes passed overhead every year. One day, in August 1983, Kaczynski set out hiking towards his favourite wild place:

> The best place, to me, was the largest remnant of this plateau that dates from the Tertiary age. It's kind of

rolling country, not flat, and when you get to the edge of it you find these ravines that cut very steeply in to cliff-like drop-offs and there was even a waterfall there ... That summer there were too many people around my cabin so I decided I needed some peace. I went back to the plateau and when I got there I found they had put a road right through the middle of it ... You just can't imagine how upset I was. It was from that point on I decided that, rather than trying to acquire further wilderness skills, I would work on getting back at the system. Revenge.

I can identify with pretty much every word of this, including, sometimes, the last one. This is the other reason that I do not want to end up being convinced by Kaczynski's position. Ted Kaczynski was known to the FBI as the 'Unabomber' during the twenty years in which he sent parcel bombs from his shack to those he deemed responsible for the promotion of the technological society he despises. In those two decades he killed three people and injured twenty-three others. His targets lost eyes and fingers and sometimes their lives. He nearly brought down an aeroplane. Unlike many other critics of the technosphere, who are busy churning out books and doing the lecture circuit and updating their anarcho-primitivist websites, Kaczynski wasn't just theorising about being a revolutionary. He meant it.

*

Back to the scythe. It's an ancient piece of technology; tried and tested, improved and honed, literally and metaphorically, over centuries. It's what the green thinkers of the 1970s used to call an 'appropriate technology' – a phrase that I would love to see resurrected – and what the unjustly neglected philosopher Ivan Illich called a 'tool for conviviality'. Illich's critique of technology, like Kaczynski's, was really a critique of power. Advanced technologies, he explained, created dependency; they took tools and processes out of the hands of individuals and put them into the metaphorical hands of organisations. The result was often 'modernised poverty' in which human individuals became the equivalent of parts in a machine rather than owners and users of a tool. In exchange for flashing lights and throbbing engines, they lost the thing that should be most valuable to a human individual: autonomy. Freedom. Control.

Illich's critique did not, of course, just apply to technology. It applied more widely to social and economic life. A few years back I wrote a book called *Real England*, which was also about conviviality, as it turned out. In particular, it was about how human-scale, vernacular ways of life in my home country were disappearing, victims of the march of the machine. Small shops were crushed by supermarkets, family farms pushed out of business by the global agricultural market, ancient orchards rooted up for housing developments, pubs shut down by developers and state interference. What the book turned out to be about, again, was autonomy and control: about the need for people to be in control of their tools and places rather than to remain cogs in the machine.

Critics of that book called it nostalgic and conservative, as they do with all books like it. They confused a desire for human-scale autonomy, and for the independent character, quirkiness, mess and creativity that usually results, with a desire to retreat to some imagined 'Golden Age'. It's a familiar criticism, and a lazy and boring one. Nowadays, when I'm faced with digs like this I like to quote E. F. Schumacher, who replied to the accusation that he was a 'crank' by saying, 'A crank is a very elegant device. It's small, it's strong, it's lightweight, energy efficient, and it makes revolutions.'

Still, if I'm honest, I'll have to concede that the critics may have been onto something in one sense. If you want human-scale living, you doubtless do need to look backwards. If there was an age of human autonomy, it seems to me that it probably is behind us. It is certainly not ahead of us, or not for a very long time; not unless we change course, which we show no sign of wanting to do.

Schumacher's riposte reminds us that Ivan Illich was far from being the only thinker to advance a critique of the dehumanising impacts of mega-technologies on both the human soul and the human body. E. F. Schumacher, Leopold Kohr, Neil Postman, Jacques Ellul, Lewis Mumford, Kirkpatrick Sale, Jerry Mander, Edward Goldsmith – there's a long roll-call of names, thinkers and doers all, promoters of appropriate energy and convivial tools, interrogators of the paradigm. For a while, in the 1960s and 1970s, they were riding high. Then they were buried, by Thatcher and Reagan, by three decades of cheap oil and shopping. Lauded as visionaries at first, at least by some, they became mocked as throwbacks by those who remembered them. Kaczynski's pipe bombs, plugged with whittled wood, wired up to batteries and hidden inside books, were a futile attempt to spark a revolution from the ashes of their thinking. He will spend the rest of his life in Colorado's Federal Administrative Maximum Facility Penitentiary as a result – surely one of the least human-scale and convivial places on Earth.

But things change. Today, as three decades of cheap fuel, free money and economic enclosure come to a shuddering, collapsing halt, suddenly it's Thatcher and Reagan, and the shrieking, depleting faithful in the Friedmanite think tanks, who are starting to look like the throwbacks. Another orthodoxy is in its death throes. What happens next is what interests me, and worries me too.

*

Every summer I run scything courses in the north of England and in Scotland. I teach the skills I've picked up using this tool over the past five or six years to people who have never used one before. It's probably the most fulfilling thing I do, in the all-round sense, apart from being a father to my children (and scything is easier than fathering). Writing is fulfilling too, intellectually and sometimes emotionally, but physically it is draining and boring: hours in front of computers or scribbling notes in books, or reading and thinking or attempting to think.

Mowing with a scythe shuts down the jabbering brain for a little while, or at least the rational part of it, leaving only the primitive part, the intuitive reptile consciousness, working fully. Using a scythe properly is a meditation; your body in tune with the tool, your tool in tune with the land. You concentrate without thinking, you follow the lay of the ground with the face of your blade, you are aware of the keenness of its edge, you can hear the birds, see things moving through the grass ahead of you. Everything is connected to everything else, and if it isn't, it doesn't work: your blade tip jams into the ground, you blunt the edge on a molehill you didn't notice, you pull a muscle in your back, you slice your finger as you're honing. Focus – relaxed focus – is the key to mowing well. Tolstoy, who obviously wrote from experience, explained it in *Anna Karenina*:

> The longer Levin went on mowing, the oftener he experienced those moments of oblivion when his arm no longer seemed to swing the scythe, but the scythe itself his whole body, so conscious and full of life; and as if by magic, regularly and definitely without thought being given to it, the work accomplished itself of its own accord. These were blessed moments.

People come on my courses for all kinds of reasons, but most want to learn to use the tool for a practical purpose. Sometimes they are managing wildlife reserves or golf courses. Some of them want to control sedge grass or nettles or brambles in their fields or gardens, or destroy couch grass on their allotments. Some of them want to trim lawns or verges. This year I'm also doing some courses for people with mental health problems, using tools to help them root themselves in practical, calming work.

Still, the reaction of most people when I tell them I'm a scythe teacher is the same: incredulity or amusement, or polite interest, usually overlaid onto a sense that this is something quaint and rather silly that doesn't have much place in the modern world. After all, we have strimmers and lawnmowers now, and they are noisier than scythes and have buttons and use electricity or petrol and therefore they must perform better, right?

Now, I would say this of course, but no, it is not right. Certainly if you have a five-acre meadow and you want to cut the grass for hay or silage, you are going to get it done a lot quicker (though not necessarily more efficiently) with a tractor and cutter bar than you would with a scythe team, which is the way it was done before the 1950s. Down at the human scale, though, the scythe still reigns supreme.

A growing number of people I teach, for example, are looking for an alternative to a brushcutter. A brushcutter is essentially a mechanical scythe. It is a great heavy piece of machinery that needs to be operated with both hands and requires its user to dress up like Darth Vader in order to swing it through the grass. It roars like a motorbike, belches out fumes and requires a regular diet of fossil fuels. It hacks through the grass instead of slicing it cleanly like a scythe blade. It is more cumbersome, more dangerous, no faster and far less pleasant to use than the tool it replaced. And yet you see it used everywhere: on motorway verges by council workers, in parks by municipal gardeners; even, for heaven's sake, in nature reserves. It's a horrible, clumsy, ugly, noisy, inefficient thing. So why do people use it, and why do they still laugh at the scythe?

To ask that question in those terms is to misunderstand what is going on. Brushcutters are not used instead of scythes because they are better; they are used because their use is conditioned by our attitudes to technology. Performance is not really the point, and neither is efficiency. Religion is the point; the religion of complexity. The myth of progress manifested in tool form. Plastic is better than wood. Moving parts are better than fixed parts. Noisy things are better than quiet things. Complicated things are better than simple things. New things are better than old things. We all believe this, whether we like it or not. It's how we were brought up.

*

The homely, pipe-smoking, cob-and-straw visions of Illich and Schumacher take us back to what we would like to think was a kinder time; a time when no one was posting bombs out in pursuit of a gentler world. This was the birth of what would become known as the 'green' movement. I sometimes like to say that the movement was born in the same year as me – 1972, the year in which the fabled *Limits to Growth* report was published by the Club of Rome – and this is near enough to the truth to be a jumping-off point for a narrative.

If the green movement was born in the early 1970s, then the 1980s, when there were whales to be saved and rainforests to be campaigned for, were its adolescence. Its coming-of-age party was in 1992, in the Brazilian city of Rio de Janeiro. The 1992 Earth Summit was a jamboree of promises and commitments: to tackle climate change, to protect forests, to protect biodiversity and to promote something called 'sustainable development', a new concept that would become, over the next two decades, the most fashionable in global politics and business. The future looked bright for the greens back then. It often does when you're twenty.

Two decades on, things look rather different. This year, the bureaucrats, the activists and the ministers gathered again in Rio for a stock-taking exercise called 'Rio +20'.

It was accompanied by the usual shrill demands for optimism and hope, but there was no disguising the hollowness of the exercise. Every environmental problem identified at the original Earth Summit has got worse in the intervening twenty years, often very much worse, and there is no sign of this changing.

The green movement, which seemed to be carrying all before it in the early 1990s, has plunged into a full-on midlife crisis. Unable to significantly change either the system or the behaviour of the public, assailed by a rising movement of 'sceptics' and by public boredom with being hectored about carbon and consumption, colonised by a new breed of corporate spivs for whom 'sustainability' is just another opportunity for selling things, the greens are seeing a nasty realisation dawn: despite all their work, their passion, their commitment and the fact that most of what they have been saying has been broadly right – they are losing. There is no likelihood of the world going their way. In most green circles now, sooner or later, the conversation comes round to the same question: what the hell do we do next?

There are plenty of people who think they know the answer to that question. One of them is Peter Kareiva, who would like to think that he and his kind represent the future of environmentalism, and who may turn out to be right. Kareiva is chief scientist of the Nature Conservancy, an American NGO that claims to be the world's largest environmental organisation. He is a scientist, a revisionist and one among a growing number of former greens who might best be called 'neo-environmentalists'.

The resemblance between this coalescing group and the Friedmanite 'neo-liberals' of the early 1970s is intriguing.

Like the neo-liberals, the neo-environmentalists are attempting to break through the lines of an old orthodoxy that is visibly exhausted and confused. Like the neo-liberals, they are mostly American and mostly male and they emphasise scientific measurement and economic analysis over other ways of seeing and measuring. Like the neo-liberals, they cluster around a few key think tanks: then, the Institute of Economic Affairs, the Cato Institute and the Adam Smith Institute; now, the Breakthrough Institute, the Long Now Foundation and the Copenhagen Consensus. Like the neo-liberals, they are beginning to grow in numbers at a time of global collapse and uncertainty. And, like the neo-liberals, they think they have radical solutions.

Kareiva's ideas are a good place to start in understanding them. He is an outspoken former conservationist who now believes that most of what the greens think they know is wrong. Nature, he says, is more resilient than fragile; science proves it. 'Humans degrade and destroy and crucify the natural environment,' he says, 'and 80 per cent of the time it recovers pretty well.' Wilderness does not exist; all of it has been influenced by humans at some time. Trying to protect large functioning ecosystems from human development is mostly futile; humans like development, and you can't stop them having it. Nature is tough and will adapt to this: 'Today, coyotes roam downtown Chicago and peregrines astonish San Franciscans as they sweep down skyscraper canyons . . . as we destroy habitats, we create new ones.' Now that 'science' has shown us that nothing is 'pristine' and nature 'adapts', there's no reason to worry about many traditional green goals such as, for example, protecting rainforest habitats. 'Is halting deforestation in the Amazon . . . feasible?' he asks. 'Is it even necessary?' Somehow, you know what the answer is going to be before he gives it to you.

If this sounds like the kind of thing that a US Republican presidential candidate might come out with, that's because it is. But Kareiva is not alone. Variations on this line have recently been pushed by the US thinker Stewart Brand, the British writer Mark Lynas, the Danish anti-green poster boy Bjørn Lomborg and the American writers Emma Marris, Ted Nordhaus and Michael Schellenberger. They in turn are building on work done in the past by other self-declared green 'heretics' like Richard D. North and Wilfred Beckerman.

Beyond the field of conservation, the neo-environmentalists are distinguished by their attitude to new technologies, which they almost uniformly see as positive. Civilisation, nature and people can be 'saved' only by enthusiastically embracing biotechnology, synthetic biology, nuclear power, geoengineering and anything else with the prefix 'new' that annoys Greenpeace. The traditional green focus on 'limits' is dismissed as naive. We are now, in Brand's words, 'as Gods', and we have to step up and accept our responsibility to manage the planet rationally through the use of new technology guided by enlightened science.

Neo-environmentalists also tend to exhibit an excitable enthusiasm for markets. They like to put a price on things like trees, lakes, mist, crocodiles, rainforests and watersheds, all of which can deliver 'ecosystem services', which can be bought and sold, measured and totted up. Tied in with this is an almost religious attitude to the scientific method. Everything that matters can be measured by science and priced by markets, and any claims without numbers attached can be easily dismissed. This is presented as 'pragmatism' but is actually something rather different: an attempt to exclude from the green debate any interventions based on morality, emotion, intuition, spiritual connection or simple human feeling.

Some of this might be shocking to some old-guard greens – which is the point – but it is hardly a new message. In fact, it is a very old one; it is simply a variant on the old Wellsian techno-optimism that has been promising us cornucopia for over a century. It's an old-fashioned Big Science, Big Tech and Big Money narrative, filtered through the lens of the internet and garlanded with holier-than-thou talk about saving the poor and feeding the world.

But though they burn with the shouty fervour of the born-again, the neo-environmentalists are not exactly wrong. In fact, they are at least half right. They are right to say that the human-scale, convivial approaches of those 1970s thinkers are never going to work if the world continues to formulate itself according to the demands of late-capitalist industrialism. They are right to say that a world of 9 billion people all seeking the status of middle-class consumers cannot be sustained by vernacular approaches. They are right to say that the human impact on the planet is enormous and irreversible. They are right to say that traditional conservation efforts sometimes idealised a pre-industrial nature. They are right to say that the campaigns of green NGOs often exaggerate and dissemble. And they are right to say that the greens have hit a wall, and that continuing to ram their heads against it is not going to knock it down.

What's interesting, though, is what they go on to build on this foundation. The first sign that this is not, as declared, a simple 'eco-pragmatism' but is something rather different, comes when you read paragraphs like this:

> For decades people have unquestioningly accepted the idea that our goal is to preserve nature in its pristine, pre-human state. But many scientists have come to see this as an outdated dream that thwarts bold new plans to save the environment and prevents us from having a fuller relationship with nature.

This is the PR blurb for Emma Marris's book *Rambunctious Garden: Saving Nature in a Post-Wild World*, though it could just as easily be from anywhere else in the neo-environmentalist canon. But who are the 'people' who have 'unquestioningly accepted' this line? I've met a lot of conservationists and environmentalists in my time and I don't think I've ever met one who believed there was any such thing as 'pristine, pre-human' nature. What they did believe was that there were still large-scale, functioning ecosystems that were worth getting out of bed to protect from destruction.

To understand why, consider the case of the Amazon. What do we value about the Amazon forest? Do people seek to protect it because they believe it is 'pristine' and 'pre-human'? Clearly not, since it's inhabited and harvested by large numbers of tribal people, some of whom have been there for millennia. The Amazon is not important because it is 'untouched'; it's important because it is wild, in the sense that it is self-willed. It is lived in and from by humans, but it is not created or controlled by them. It teems with a great, shifting, complex diversity of both human and non-human life, and no species dominates the mix. It is a complex, working eco-system that is also a human-culture system, because, in any kind of worthwhile world, the two are linked.

This is what intelligent green thinking has always called for: human and non-human nature working in some degree of harmony, in a modern world of compromise and change in which some principles, nevertheless, are worth cleaving to. 'Nature' is a resource for people, and always has been; we all have to eat, make shelter, hunt, live from its bounty like any other creature. But that doesn't preclude us understanding that it has a practical, cultural, emotional and even spiritual value beyond that too, which is equally necessary for our well-being.

The neo-environmentalists, needless to say, have no time for this kind of fluff. They have a great big straw man to build up and knock down, and once they've got that out of the way, they can move on to the really important part of their message. Here's Kareiva, giving us the money shot in *Breakthrough Journal* with fellow authors Michelle Marvier and Robert Lalasz:

> Instead of pursuing the protection of biodiversity for biodiversity's sake, a new conservation should seek to enhance those natural systems that benefit the widest number of people . . . Conservation will measure its achievement in large part by its relevance to people.

There it is, in black and white: the wild is dead, and what remains of nature is for people. We can effectively do what we like, and we should. Science says so! A full circle has been drawn: the greens have been buried by their own children, and under the soil with them has gone their naive, romantic and anti-scientific belief that non-human life has any value beyond what we very modern humans can make use of.

'Wilderness can be saved permanently', claims Ted Kaczynski, 'only by eliminating the techno-industrial system.' I am beginning to think that the neo-environmentalists may leave a deliciously ironic legacy: proving the Unabomber right.

*

In his book *A Short History of Progress*, Ronald Wright coins the term 'progress trap'. A progress trap, says Wright, is a short-term social or technological improvement that turns out in the longer term to be a backward step. By the time this is realised – if it ever is – it is too late to change course.

The earliest example he gives is the improvement in hunting techniques in the Upper Palaeolithic era, around fifteen thousand years ago. Wright tracks the disappearance of wildlife on a vast scale whenever prehistoric humans arrived on a new continent. As Wright explains: 'Some of their slaughter sites were almost industrial in size: 1000 mammoths at one; more than 100,000 horses at another.' But there was a catch:

The perfection of hunting spelled the end of hunting as a way of life. Easy meat meant more babies. More babies meant more hunters. More hunters, sooner or later, meant less game. Most of the great human migrations across the world at this time must have been driven by want, as we bankrupted the land with our moveable feasts.

This is the progress trap. Each improvement in our knowledge or in our technology will create new problems, which require new improvements. Each of these improvements tends to make society bigger, more complex, less human-scale, more destructive of non-human life and more likely to collapse under its own weight.

Spencer Wells takes up the story in his book *Pandora's Seed*, a revisionist history of the development of agriculture. The story we were all taught at school – or I was, anyway – is that humans 'developed' or 'invented' agriculture, because they were clever enough to see that it would form the basis of a better way of living than hunting and gathering. This is the same attitude that makes us assume that a brushcutter is a better way of mowing grass than a scythe, and it seems to be equally erroneous. As Wells demonstrates, analysis of the skeletal remains of people living before and after the transition to agriculture during the Palaeolithic demonstrate something remarkable: an all-round collapse in quality of life when farming was adopted.

Hunter-gatherers living during the Palaeolithic period, between 30,000 and 9000 BC, were on average taller – and thus, we can infer, healthier – than any people since, including people living in late twentieth-century America. Their median lifespan was longer than at any period for the next six thousand years, and their health, as estimated by measuring the pelvic inlet depth of their skeletons, appears to have been better, again, than at any period since – including the present day. This collapse in individual well-being was likely due to the fact that settled agricultural life is physically harder and more disease-ridden than the life of a shifting hunter-gatherer community.

So much for progress. But why in this case, Wells asks, would any community move from hunting-gathering to agriculture? The answer seems to be: not because they wanted to, but because they had to. They had spelled the end of their hunting-gathering lifestyle by getting too good at it. They had killed off most of their prey and expanded their numbers beyond the point at which they could all survive. They had fallen into a progress trap.

We have been falling into them ever since. Look at the proposals of the neo-environmentalists in this light and you can see them as a series of attempts to dig us out of the progress traps that their predecessors knocked us into. Genetically modified crops, for example, are regularly sold to us as a means of 'feeding the world'. But why is the world hungry? At least in part because of the previous wave of agricultural improvements – the so-called 'Green Revolution', which between the 1940s and 1970s promoted a new form of agriculture that depended on high levels of pesticides and herbicides, new agricultural technologies and high-yielding strains of crops. The Green Revolution is trumpeted by progressives as having supposedly 'fed a billion people' who would otherwise have starved. And maybe it did; but then we had to keep feeding them – or should I say us? – and our children. In the meantime it had been discovered that the pesticides and herbicides were killing off vast swathes of wildlife, and the high-yield monoculture crops were wrecking both the health of the soil and the crop diversity that in previous centuries had helped prevent the spread of disease and the likelihood of crop failure.

It is in this context that we now have to listen to lectures from the neo-environmentalists and others insisting that GM crops are a moral obligation if we want to feed the world and save the planet: precisely the arguments that were made last time around. GM crops are an attempt to solve the problems caused by the last progress trap; they are also the next one. I would be willing to bet a lot of money that in forty years' time, the successors of the neo-environmentalists will be making precisely the same arguments about the necessity of adopting the next wave of technologies needed to dig us out of the trap that GM crops have dropped us neatly into. Perhaps it will be vat-grown meat, or synthetic wheat or some nano-bio-gubbins as yet unthought of. Either way, it will be vital for growth and progress, and a moral necessity. As Kurt Vonnegut would have said, 'So it goes.'

Where will this end, assuming it ever does? The late American wilderness writer Edward Abbey is mocked by Peter Kareiva for supposedly romanticising the time he spent alone in the deserts, forests and rivers of the United States in the middle of the twentieth century. Abbey had committed the cardinal sin of writing powerfully about an emotional response to nature. Still, if I were forced to choose between the two men's views of where this was all leading, I'd choose Abbey's any day. He saw us sleepwalking towards a future that was:

> . . . nuclear-powered, computer-directed, firmly and thoroughly policed. Call it the Anthill State, the Beehive Society, a technocratic despotism – perhaps benevolent, perhaps not, but in either case the enemy of personal liberty, family independence and community sovereignty, shutting off for a long time to come the

freedom to choose among alternate ways of living.
The domination of nature made possible by misapplied
science leads to the domination of people; to a dreary
and totalitarian uniformity . . .

'Romanticising the past' is a familiar accusation, made
mostly by people who think it is more grown up to romanticise the future. But it's not necessary to convince yourself
that Palaeolithic hunter-gatherers lived in paradise in order
to observe that progress is a ratchet, every turn forcing us
more tightly into the gears of a machine we were forced to
create to solve the problems created by progress. It is far too
late to think about dismantling this machine in a rational
manner – and in any case who wants to? We can't deny that
it brings benefits to us, even as it chokes us and our world
by degrees. Those benefits are what keep us largely quiet
and uncomplaining as the machine rolls on, in the words of
the poet R. S. Thomas, 'over the creeds and masterpieces':

> . . . *The machine appeared*
> *In the distance, singing to itself*
> *Of money. Its song was the web*
> *They were caught in, men and women*
> *Together. The villages were as flies*
> *To be sucked empty.*
> *God secreted*
> *A tear. Enough, enough,*
> *He commanded, but the machine*
> *Looked at him and went on singing.*

*

Over the next few years, the old green movement that I grew up with is likely to fall to pieces. Many of those pieces will be picked up and hoarded by the growing ranks of the neo-environmentalists. The mainstream of the green movement has laid itself open to their advances in recent years with its obsessive focus on carbon and energy technologies and its refusal to speak up for a subjective, vernacular, non-technical engagement with nature. The neo-environmentalists have a great advantage over the old greens, with their threatening talk about limits to growth, behaviour change and other such against-the-grain stuff: they are telling this civilisation what it wants to hear. What it wants to hear is that the progress trap that our civilisation is caught in can be escaped from by inflating a green tech bubble on which we can sail merrily into the future, happy as gods and equally in control.

In the short term, the future belongs to the neo-environmentalists, and it is going to be painful to watch. In the long term, though, I'd guess they will fail, for two reasons. Firstly, that bubbles always burst. Our civilisation is beginning to break down. We are at the start of an unfolding economic and social collapse that may take decades or centuries to play out – and which is playing out against the background of a planetary ecocide which nobody seems able to prevent. We are not gods, and our machines will not get us off this hook, however clever they are and however much we would like to believe it.

But there is another reason that the new breed are unlikely to be able to build the world they want to see: we are not – even they are not – primarily rational, logical or 'scientific' beings. Our human relationship to the rest of nature is not akin to the analysis of bacteria in a petri dish; it is more like the complex, love–hate relationship we might have with lovers or parents or siblings. It is who we are, unspoken and felt and frustrating and inspiring and vital and impossible to peer-review. You can reach part of it with the analytical mind, but the rest will remain buried in the ancient woodland floor of human evolution and in the depth of our old ape brains, which see in pictures and think in stories. Civilisation has always been a project of control, but you can't win a war against the wild within yourself.

Is it possible to read the words of someone like Theodore Kaczynski and be convinced by the case he makes, even as you reject what he did with the knowledge? Is it possible to look at human cultural evolution as a series of progress traps, the latest of which you are caught in like a fly on a sundew, with no means of escape? Is it possible to observe the unfolding human attack on nature with horror, be determined to do whatever you can to stop it, and at the same time know that much of it cannot be stopped, whatever you do? Is it possible to see the future as dark and darkening further; to reject false hope and desperate pseudo-optimism without collapsing into despair?

It's going to have to be, because it's where I am right now. But where do I go next? What do I do? Between Kaczynski and Kareiva, what can I find to alight on that will still hold my weight?

I'm not sure I know the answer. But I know there is no going back to anything. And I know that we are not headed, now, towards convivial tools. We are not headed towards human-scale development. This culture is about superstores, not little shops, synthetic biology not local community, brushcutters not scythes. This is a culture that develops new life forms first and asks questions later; a species that is in the process of, in the words of the poet Robinson Jeffers, 'break[ing] its legs on its own cleverness'.

What does the near future look like? I'd put my bets on a strange and unworldly combination of an ongoing collapse that will continue to fragment both nature and culture, and a new wave of techno-green 'solutions' being unveiled in a doomed attempt to prevent it. I don't believe now that anything can break this cycle, bar some kind of reset: the kind that we have seen many times before in human history. Some kind of fall back down to a lower level of civilisational complexity. Something like the storm that is now visibly brewing all around us.

If you don't like any of this, but you know you can't stop it, where does it leave you? The answer is that it leaves you with an obligation to be honest about where you are in history's great cycle, and what you have the power to do and what you don't. If you think you can magic us out of the progress trap with new ideas or new technologies, you are wasting your time. If you think that the usual 'campaigning' behaviour is going to work today where it didn't work yesterday, you will be wasting your time. If you think the machine can be reformed, tamed or defanged, you will be wasting your time. If you draw up a great big plan for a better world based on science and rational argument, you will be wasting your time. If you try to live in the past, you will be wasting your time. If you romanticise hunter-gathering or send bombs to computer-store owners, you will be wasting your time.

And so I come to this point, and I ask myself: what, at this moment in history, would not be a waste of my time? And I arrive at five tentative answers.

One: Withdrawing. If you do this, a lot of people will call you a 'defeatist' or a 'doomer', or claim you are 'burned out'. They will tell you that you have an obligation to work for climate justice or world peace or the end of bad things everywhere, and that 'fighting' is always better than 'quitting'. Ignore them, and take part in a very ancient practical and spiritual tradition: withdrawing from the fray. Withdraw not with cynicism, but with a questing mind. Withdraw so that you can allow yourself to sit back quietly and feel – intuit – work out what is right for you, and what nature might need from you. Withdraw because refusing to help the machine advance – refusing to tighten the ratchet further – is a deeply moral position. Withdraw because action is not always more effective than inaction. Withdraw to examine your worldview: the cosmology, the paradigm, the assumptions, the direction of travel. All real change starts with withdrawal.

Two: Preserving non-human life. The revisionists will continue to tell us that wildness is dead, nature is for people and Progress is God, and they will continue to be wrong. There is still much remaining of the Earth's wild diversity, but it may not remain for much longer. The human empire is the greatest threat to what remains of life on Earth, and you are part of it. What can you do – really do, at a practical level – about this? Maybe you can buy up some land and re-wild it; maybe you can let your garden run free; maybe you can work for a conservation group or set one up yourself; maybe you can put your body in the way of a bulldozer;

maybe you can use your skills to prevent the destruction of yet another wild place. How can you create or protect a space for non-human nature to breathe easier; how can you give something that isn't *us* a chance to survive our appetites?

Three: Getting your hands dirty. Root yourself in something: some practical work, some place, some way of doing. Pick up your scythe or your equivalent and get out there and do physical work in clean air surrounded by things you cannot control. Get away from your laptop and throw away your smartphone, if you have one. Ground yourself in things and places, learn or practise human-scale convivial skills. Only by doing that, rather than just talking about it, do you learn what is real and what's not, and what makes sense and what is so much hot air.

Four: Insisting that nature has a value beyond utility. And telling everyone. Remember that you are one lifeform among many and understand that everything has intrinsic value. If you want to call this 'ecocentrism' or 'deep ecology', do it. If you want to call it something else, do that. If you want to look to tribal societies for your inspiration, do it. If that seems too gooey, just look up into the sky. Sit on the grass, and touch a tree trunk, walk into the hills, dig the garden, look at what you find in the soil, marvel at what the hell this thing called *life* could possibly be. Value it for what it is, try to understand what it is, and have nothing but pity or contempt for people who tell you that its only value is in what they can extract from it.

Five: Building refuges. The coming decades are likely to challenge much of what we think we know about what progress is, and about who we are in relation to the rest of nature. Advanced technologies will challenge our sense of what it means to be human at the same time as the tide of extinction rolls on. The ongoing collapse of social and economic infrastructures, and of the web of life itself, will kill off much of what we value. In this context, ask yourself: what power do you have to preserve what is of value – creatures, skills, things, places? Can you work, with others or alone, to create places or networks that act as refuges from the unfolding storm? Can you think, or act, like the librarian of a monastery through the Dark Ages, guarding the old books as empires rise and fall outside?

It will be apparent by now that for the last five paragraphs I have been talking to myself.

These are the things that make sense to me right now, when I think about what is coming and what I can do, still, with some joy and determination. If you don't feel despair, in times like these, you are not fully alive. But there has to be something beyond despair too; or rather, something that accompanies it, like a companion on the road. This is my approach, right now. It is, I suppose, the development of a personal philosophy for a dark time; a dark ecology. None of it is going to save the world – but then there is no saving the world, and the ones who say there is are the ones you need to save it from.

*

For now, I've had enough of writing. My head is buzzing with it. I am going to pick up my new scythe, lovingly made for me recently from sugar maple, a beautiful object in itself, which I can just look at for hours. I am going to pick it up and go out and find some grass to mow.

I am going to cut great swathes of it, my blade gliding through the vegetation, leaving it in elegant curving wind-rows behind me. I am going to walk ahead, following the ground, emptying my head, managing the land, not like a god but like a tenant. I am going to breathe the still-clean air and listen to the still-singing birds and reflect on the fact that the Earth is older and harder than the machine that is eating it – that it is indeed more resilient than fragile – and that change comes quickly when it comes, and that knowledge is not the same as wisdom.

A scythe is an old tool, but it has changed through its millennia of existence, changed and adapted as all life does. Like a microchip or a combustion engine it is a technology that has allowed us to manipulate and control our environment, and to accelerate the rate of that manipulation and control. A scythe, too, is a progress trap. But it is limited enough in its speed and application to allow that control to be rolled out in a way that is understandable by, and accountable to, individual human beings. It is a compromise we can control, as much as we can ever control anything; a stage on the journey we can still understand.

There is always change, as a neo-environmentalist would happily tell you; but there are different qualities of change. There is human-scale change and there is industrial-scale change; there is change led by the needs of complex systems and change led by the needs of individual humans. There is a manageable rate of evolution and there is a chaotic, excitable rush towards shiny things perched on the edge of a great ravine, flashing and scrolling like sirens in the gathering dusk.

When you have mown a hayfield, you should turn and look back on your work admiringly. If you have got it right, you should see a field lined with long, curving windrows of cut grass, with clean, mown strips between them. It's a beautiful sight, which would have been familiar to every medieval citizen of this old, old continent. If you were up at dawn, mowing in the dew – the best time, and the traditional one to cut for hay – you should leave the windrows to dry in the sun, then go down the rows with a pitchfork later in the day and turn them over. Leave the other side of the rows to dry until the sun has done its work, then come back and 'ted' the grass – spread it out evenly across the field. Dry it for a few hours or a few days, depending on the weather, then come back and turn it over again. Give it as much time as it needs to dry in the sun.

After that, if the rain has held off, you're ready to take in the hay.

Dark Mountain, issue 3, 2013

III : CONNECTION

In the Black Chamber

What I know of the divine sciences and Holy Scripture,
I learnt in woods and fields. I have had no other masters
than the beeches and the oaks.
St Bernard

Here is life without God. Just look at it!
George Orwell

It is a long walk, or it seems like one, especially if you are
taking your small children with you. In reality, it is just over
a kilometre; a journey that, on the surface, would take ten
minutes or so. But we are not on the surface. We are several
hundred feet below the slopes of a limestone mountain, and
if we weren't all carrying torches, the darkness would be
entire and unending.

This is Grotte de Niaux – Niaux cave – in the French Pyr-
enees. The great rock overhang that marks the entrance is
visible for miles along the river valley outside. The cave is
a scribbled network of tunnels, most of them inaccessible
now, at least to the public. As you move past the artificial entrance passage, through the thick steel door, which is locked
every night, your torchlight hits stalagmites three times the
height of a human being, vast bulges and excrescences of
rock on the ceiling and walls, dark crevices leading to cham-
bers and side passages, icy black lakes and all the beauty and

solidity to be found in the guts of an old mountain. It is cool, even and blacker than anything under the stars.

Our guide walks us slowly through the network of passages, sometimes slowing for us to skirt around an underground lake, at other times warning us of the need to crouch or watch our footing on the slippery ground. She stops at a few familiar points along the way to show us particular marks on the walls. The anticipation is palpable.

Time moves strangely in a cave. How long it takes us to get to the endpoint in our journey is hard to say. I have no watch. It certainly takes longer than I had imagined it might, and the walk is harder than I would have thought. But when we get there, we know we have arrived.

The guide stops and shines her powerful torch upwards. We can see nothing beyond our beams, but we can sense the size of this place. Everything has opened out. It is a strange and intimidating feeling.

'This is *le Salon noir*,' says the guide. 'In English, the Black Chamber.'

We all stand for a minute waving our torches in all directions, trying to get a sense of this place and its meaning. Its walls are great sheets of rock that look as if they have been melted and then folded in on each other. There is a silver sheen to them. As we begin to judge its size and scale, we can see that we are standing in an enormous domed chamber: an underground St Peter's or St Paul's. I am struck by this comparison as I crane my neck to try to gauge the height of the roof. Was this a holy place? Do the domes we construct now above the ground – the cathedrals, gurdwaras, mosques and temples – come down in a direct lineage from places like this?

'Can anybody sing?' asks the guide. We look down at our feet and mumble. Most of us are English. The guide moves to the centre of the chamber and sings a few notes. They hang in the air for a moment, the acoustics near perfect.

'Did people come here because of this?' she asks. 'Did people sing here? Was there performance? We can know none of these things. Now, I am going to ask you all to turn off your torches, and put them down, here on this rock. Then I am going to ask you to follow me.'

The guide moves over to one of the walls. In almost total darkness our small group clusters around her. She picks up her torch, which has been lying on the ground, and angles it upwards to a point on the wall. There is an audible collective gasp, which echoes around the Black Chamber, as the image appears in her beam.

'Here', she says, 'we can see a group of bison.'

The painting on the wall is probably around fifteen thousand years old, a product of the Palaeolithic era, before the end of the last ice age brought about the great climatic shift that turned humans – through choice or necessity? – away from hunting and towards farming. The people who painted these creatures, with simple, black pigment on the walls, are classified by prehistoric anthropologists as 'Magdalenians'. They were hunters and gatherers who lived in this part of southern Europe between eighteen thousand and ten thousand years ago. They lived in shifting encampments, their days mapped out by the routes along which they followed the great mammals around the valleys, probably returning to this place year after year. They never lived in these caves – no one ever lived in deep caves, which are cold, dark and wet. But they came here, all this way, into the depths of the mountain, with only tiny, guttering candles to guide them, to paint the animals.

All around the walls of the Black Chamber are hundreds of line drawings depicting great mammals: herds of bison, pairs of mammoths, groups of ibex. They are painted elegantly, sweepingly, and with clear expertise. Whoever drew these creatures was not doing it for the first time: these were artists who knew their work well. They also knew the animals: the anatomical detail is finely observed, right down to the beards on the ibex and the anal flaps on the mammoths.

There are many caves like Niaux across southern France and northern Spain. In some of them are also found handprints, the occasional depiction of a human being, line-and-dot markings that may be some kind of language but that cannot be interpreted. Sometimes, incredibly, the paint-boxes of these people remain below the walls they painted on, as do the candles they used to light them. All this after 150 centuries.

What was this, and why did it happen? We have few clues. We know little about these people – or at least, little about their worldview. What was the world, to them, and what spirits haunted it? What stories did they tell about their place here, about the past and present? Who, what, did they think they were? We don't know, and we never will.

But we have the cave paintings, and within them, some themes are common. For example, these are not, as they are often referred to, 'hunting scenes'. In none of these drawings, in none of these caves, is there any sign of violence. There are no hunters and no weapons. In any case, these animals seem not to have been hunted at all. Analysis of bones from Magdalenian camps shows that their main meat source was reindeer. There are no reindeer on the walls. These people seem not to have hunted the creatures they painted, or to have painted the creatures they hunted. These are not triumphant paintings of vanquished prey.

So why paint them? And why paint them like this: free-standing, alone or in herds, but never on the ground, never surrounded by any vegetation or depiction of their environment, and never in the presence of humans: almost as if these animals were floating, unmoored from the world?

Theories abound, of course. It has been speculated that the drawings would have been created by an elite class of artists and offered only to the cave: no one else would have seen them. It has been proposed that they were created for mass religious rites, which would have been held here. Others have suggested – and this suggestion is perhaps backed up by drawings of half-human, half-animal creatures found in some of the caves – that these were depictions of, or aids to, shamanic journeys: visits to another world in which humans became animals and animals became humans.

I'm overtaken by a number of emotions as I stand in the Black Chamber, but the one that proves impossible to shake off is a huge sense of awe: a physical sensation that I did not expect and don't quite know how to handle. It is as if something age-old and darkly powerful has descended from the roof of the cavern and settled in me and will not leave. And as I look at the paintings, and take in the sensations of being in this place, I think that perhaps I begin to understand why people were here. I don't know what they did, or who they were, but I can feel the power in the place, and it tells me why they might have come here.

It seems obvious to me – and I think the scant evidence bears it out – that whatever happened in the Black Chamber was not driven by utility. Whoever was here, and whatever they were doing, they were forging a connection to something way beyond everyday reality. These paintings are not expressions of economics or natural history. They surely sprang from the same sense of power and smallness and wonder and awe that I feel as I stand in the same place that the artists would have stood. This was a reaching out to, for, something way beyond human comprehension. This was a meeting with the sacred.

*

'Sacred', like 'spiritual', is one of those words whose meaning is easier to understand intuitively than to explain when challenged. My *Oxford English Dictionary* gives me a number of definitions, every one of them connected with religion. This isn't quite right. It's true that if you hack away from any system of religious or spiritual practice the excrescences formed by thousands of years of human idiocy, literalism and power play, you should find at its centre a tiny, delicate thing: a sacred thing. The thing that these institutions originally arose to try to touch, encircle or explain. But religions do not own the sacred; they only offer their own way of trying to approach it.

The original Latin word *sacrare* meant 'to make holy' or 'to set apart'. The *sacrum* of a temple is a holy place, which most people are not permitted to approach. Within this holy place is supposed to reside some essence of God, or of the divine. The word 'holy', which originates in the Old English word *halig*, has the same derivation as 'whole' and 'health'; it speaks of something complete, entire and unsullied.

I don't know if this helps much in explaining what I experienced in the Black Chamber, but I do know that words like 'sacred' made me uncomfortable for many years. The association with established religions on the one hand and New Age vagueness on the other tended to spur the antibodies of my university-trained mind into action. I was a teenage atheist of whom Richard Dawkins would have been proud, and even now, if I find myself dragged into a church service, I am more likely to spend my time looking for green men on the roof beams than listening to the vicar. I kick against obedience and worship and priesthoods. I don't believe in messiahs or second comings. I don't like books of rules.

But you can't approach the numinous with discursive thought, any more than you can solve an algebraic equation through the use of metaphor. 'Sell your cleverness', advises the Persian mystic poet Rumi, 'and buy bewilderment. Cleverness is mere opinion; bewilderment is intuition.' It seems like good advice, and when I try to follow it I see these things appear in a subtly different light.

When I saw God, as religions seemed to want me to see God, as an all-seeing supernatural entity with a great personal interest in my life and behaviour, laying down laws, demanding worship and promising me an afterlife in return, I had no interest, and still don't. I don't believe it. But when, later, I began to see that perhaps this was a common human interpretation of an experience of something greater than the individual ego – when I began to understand that all religions and all spiritual traditions have their mystics who had interpreted this great spirit, this Dao, this experience of the divine, very differently – then I began to see that perhaps it was something I could understand after all. I began to see that perhaps what some people call God, or the sacred, or the divine, was what I experienced as some power, some strange greatness, immanent in the wild world around me.

In other words, perhaps I do after all understand the perpetual human search for the sacred, whether I can adequately explain it or not, and I think I may know why it still matters, despite my culture's frantic attempts to convince me otherwise. I have experienced the feelings that charge the concept with so much electricity. It's just that I have never experienced them in places that people designate as holy.

Call me a heathen (I'd take it as a compliment) but for me, the 'sacred' can't be found in human things alone. This is not an intellectual or a political position; it's just how I feel, because of things I have experienced. From as early as I can remember I have regarded trees, rivers, mountains and the ocean with awe. I have had what others would call 'spiritual experiences' in all of these places. I have yelled with joy in the heart of rainforests and felt overwhelmed by something much greater than myself in deserts at midnight with no light but the stars, stars I can never see in my overdeveloped homeland.

On wild hilltops, as in the Black Chamber, I have pulled at the edges of some great force that seems way beyond me, and seems embedded in the world itself; the wild world of beauty and complexity and dark magic that my kind are busy destroying and replacing with a cold, dead culture of future-worship and straight lines. If anything is sacred, I have thought since I can remember thinking, surely it is this thing we call 'nature'.

In the Black Chamber

My late friend, the poet Glyn Hughes, told me shortly before his death that he saw the battle the environmental movement has waged over the last forty years as a 'spiritual war'. He suggested that much green campaigning, however rational its arguments may be on the surface, was spurred by a deep, atavistic need to prevent the destruction of places and things that spurred deep and powerful emotions in people.

'I'm sure it's the case that most people who get passionate about environmental matters are aghast because the world that fed those feelings is being destroyed around them,' he said, 'and they realise, after first of all being shocked by it – horrified by it – they go on to realise that it's going to make human life an impossibility. And they can see the extent to which it's motivated by greed and selfishness, and eventually come to see that it's a spiritual matter, not just a material matter.'

I had never looked at it like this, not exactly in those terms, but when Glyn said this it seemed immediately to me that he was right. Throughout my life I have had experiences on mountains and in forests that have offered up some unworded but real connection to something way beyond myself. Such experiences are very common, though we don't tend to talk about them much any more, at least in public. In his compendium of mystical traditions, *The Perennial Philosophy*, Aldous Huxley calls them 'gratuitous graces'. Wordsworth was clearly in the grip of one when he wrote in *Tintern Abbey* of

> *A motion and a spirit, that impels*
> *All thinking things, all objects of all thought,*
> *And rolls through all things.*

If the artists of the Black Chamber saw something sacred in the beasts they painted on the walls, I imagine that I see the same thing in what remains of the wild world today. A sense of the 'sacred', in other words, expresses itself to me in what Christians call Creation: in nature itself, in the self-willed places Beyond the Pale of human control.

I don't idealise this sense – or I try not to – and I don't see it as necessarily a comforting thing. I realise that what I call 'nature' (an imperfect word, but I can never seem to find a better one) is really just another word for life; an ever-turning wheel of blood and shit and death and rebirth. Nature is fatal as often as it is beautiful, and sometimes it is both at once. But, for me, that's the point: it is the fear and the violence inherent in wild nature, as much as the beauty and the peace, that inspires in me the impulses that religions ask me to direct towards their human-shaped gods: humility, a sense of smallness, sometimes a fear, usually a desire to be part of something bigger than me and my kind. To lose myself; to lose my Self.

Here, perhaps, is one reason I remain haunted by what I experienced in the Black Chamber. I imagine – I can never know, and I am glad about that – that the people who created those works of art understood the sacred through the world beyond the human. I imagine that they saw something like what I see. I imagine that they saw something more than meat and sinew in the creatures that moved around them – creatures in which god, or the sacred, or whatever you want to call this great, nameless thing, was immanent.

In much of the world even today, and certainly for the decisive majority of our human past, this sense of other-than-human nature as something thoroughly alive and intimately interwoven with human existence is and was the mainstream perception. A world without electric lights, a world without engines, is a different world entirely. It is a world that is alive. Our world of science and industry, of monocultures and monotheisms, marks a decisive shift in human seeing.

Our world is not alive; it is a machine, not an animal, and we have become starkly desensitised to the reality beyond the asphalt and the streetlights. There are no mammoths outside the entrance to Niaux today, only a car park and a gift shop. We are here now, above the ground, and above the ground is where we must live.

*

In his book *The Righteous Mind*, the psychologist Jonathan Haidt does a convincing job of demonstrating that every one of us, however much we might protest to the contrary, is a fundamentally irrational being. Much of what we believe to be 'objective', 'rational' thought, based on an examination of evidence and an assessment of verifiable facts, is in reality the result of our conscious minds fabricating ex-post-facto justifications for what our intuition has already decided to do.

Over the course of his long book, Haidt builds up a case file of evidence from neuroscience, psychology and other fields to demonstrate that the objective, rational mind, magically divorced from the clumsy, emotional physical body, is a fiction. One of the founding myths of modernity has no basis in reality. Haidt compares the relationship between intuition and reason to the relationship between the US president and his press spokesman. The spokesman's job is to explain to the world what the president has already decided to do; to rationalise it and to justify it, however unjustifiable it may sometimes be.

Our rational mind, he suggests, works in much the same way. It doesn't make the decisions: our decisions are mostly made by what we call our 'intuition'; an embodied emotional response to the world around us, which itself is conditioned by millions of years of animal evolution. Our old, animal minds are still making the running; the role of our conscious, reasoning brains is to provide the arguments to justify where they choose to go:

> We all need to take a cold hard look at the evidence
> and see reasoning for what it is . . . [it] evolved not to
> help us find truth but to help us engage in arguments,
> persuasion, and manipulation in the context of
> discussions with other people.

Part of Haidt's book builds on the earlier work of neuroscientist Antonio Damasio, who described in his own book, *Descartes' Error*, the fate of a number of his own patients who had seen the brain centres that governed emotional connection destroyed or damaged in accidents, but whose reasoning faculties remained intact. According to Enlightenment mythology, this ought to have made them perfectly rational beings, unclouded by bias or passion, able to act in accordance with evidence alone and make judgements on that basis. In reality, Damasio discovered that in every case studied, these people were unable to function as human beings. Without a feedline from the body's emotions, the reasoning mind cannot do its job. Damasio's resultant hypothesis was simple but revolutionary:

> . . . that feelings are a powerful influence on reason, that the brain systems required by the former are enmeshed in those needed by the latter, and that such specific systems are interwoven with those which regulate the body.

In our civilisation, so attached to the concept of objective rational thought, the idea that emotion and intuition may be the real basis for our actions will in many quarters be treated with horror, however obvious it might be to the untrained observer. We regard ourselves as 'progressing' away from emotion and towards reason, and we regard intuition as something primitive and therefore suspect; something to be vanquished. This, after all, is what the Enlightenment was supposed to be about: with God dispatched, human reason would remould the world in its own image.

Haidt, for one, is not convinced. He calls this 'the rationalist delusion', which he defines as:

> . . . the idea that reasoning is our most noble attribute, one that makes us like the gods (for Plato) or that brings us beyond the 'delusion' of believing in gods (for the New Atheists). The rationalist delusion is not just a claim about human nature. It's also a claim that the rational caste (philosophers or scientists) should have more power, and it usually comes along with a utopian programme for raising more rational children.

Haidt's conclusion, like Damasio's, is philosophically radical. 'Anyone who values truth', he writes, 'should stop worshipping reason.'

Neither Haidt nor Damasio are setting up a false conflict between 'reason' on the one hand and 'emotion' on the other. The case they make – and that their science makes – is much more interesting than that. Their suggestion is that the objective, rational mind – the human being as a calm, disengaged observer of an external reality – does not exist, and never can. Reason and emotion are not discrete: they are entirely enmeshed, and one cannot function properly without the other. Both, in fact, are words for the same thing: the working of different aspects of the embodied human mind.

*

Last year, a group of futurists, businessmen and scientists launched an initiative called 'Revive and Restore'. The purpose of the project was simple: to use biotechnology to revive extinct species, such as the mammoth, the aurochs and the passenger pigeon, and return them to the Earth again.

The eye-catching nature of the plans guaranteed them heady acreages of media attention across the world, virtually all of which was positive. This was partly due to the standard media assumption – common across the intellectual classes in liberal cultures – that anything involving cutting-edge technologies is inherently beneficial to humankind. It was also partly due to the fact that the originator of the project was the Californian counter-culture guru turned ecotech-booster Stewart Brand, who can play the press like his own personal fiddle and make it look easy.

Still, why not be positive about it? Brand's message seemed attractive. He wanted to make restitution, he said, for the damage humans had done to the planet. We were approaching the point where we would have the power to sequence extinct genomes and then use them to genetically modify existing species, to create near-replicas of creatures long lost to the Earth. Wouldn't that be a good thing? Imagine walking out of the cave at Niaux and seeing mammoths again in the valleys below. Who could complain about such a visionary use of our powers?

Brand is by no means alone in his support for the idea of reviving the dead. It is a concept that has been on the cards for at least a decade in various think tanks and laboratories. 'Does extinction have to be for ever?' asks Mike Archer, who runs the boldly named 'Lazarus Project' at the University of New South Wales, which claims it is on the verge of recreating an extinct breed of frog. Like Brand, he thinks not. 'De-extinction', both men say, is the future of conservation.

Though the excitement that the de-extinction prospect raised was palpable, there were some objections. Conservation biologist David Ehrenfeld was among those who pointed out that this would not be 'de-extinction' at all: the 'mammoths' it might create would not be mammoths, but elephants modified with mammoth genes. They might look like the originals, but they would be something quite new. In any case, if Brand and his ilk considered themselves to be conservationists, they should have better things to do. Given that the living African elephant is facing very real threats to its future, Ehrenfeld said, 'Why are we . . . talking about bringing back the woolly mammoth? Think about it.'

There are other objections, too. What if the science went wrong? And where exactly would you put a woolly mammoth if you 'rebuilt' one? Given that they lived in herds across vast areas of steppe, producing a single animal might be only the start of the challenges in a world of rapidly shrinking wild areas. Others worry that if 'de-extinction' becomes possible, it will provide a handy excuse for those who want reasons not to worry about causing extinctions in the first place.

Responses like this are what one commentator called the 'valid criticisms' of the de-extinction idea. That is to say, the ones that can be conceptualised and explained by the rational mind, and which are stretched on the same framework of assumptions as the original proposal. But what about the invalid criticisms? These are what interest me. I can see where Brand's idea has come from. I can understand why some people might support it. I can understand the arguments against it, too. And yet beyond and underneath all this, my reaction to the idea is much simpler and starker, and it remains once the facts have been examined on all sides. My reaction is horror.

In trying to work out why this might be, and to explain it, I am hampered by the pre-eminence, in discussions of this kind, of Haidt's 'rationalist delusion'. If you believe that all reactions ought to be 'rational', which means open to examination by calculative reason, then all reactions that stem from felt intuition, and that reason has trouble explaining, are at a disadvantage. This explains why a mystic will never win a debate with an atheist: he may have a truth on his side, but it will not be demonstrable through anything other than personal experience, and that doesn't count. Therefore, he loses.

Still, I'm not trying to convince Stewart Brand of anything; I'm just trying to understand why I feel revulsion when I hear people talking about bringing back mammoths. Writing in *Earth Island Journal* earlier this year, Jason Mark came closest to rationalising what my intuition is telling me. The de-extinctors might believe that reborn ground sloths or passenger pigeons would revive our sense of wonder at the wild world, and thus our desire to protect it, he said, but they were missing a key point:

> The Manhattan skyline at night amazes us with the scale of human invention; the Milky Way amazes us with the scale of the universe. They are both an arrangement of lights, but the first makes humanity seem huge, the second makes us feel small. The difference matters because it influences how we think about our place on this planet.

The species revivalists, says Mark, 'misunderstand what conservation is really about':

> Taking some parts of the non-human world and protecting them from our unruly desires is, above all, an exercise in restraint – not creation. Conservation is about forbearance. It's a demonstration of the discipline to leave well enough alone. Restraint, discipline, humility, forbearance. I know – these are old-fashioned virtues . . . yet they remain the essential counterweights to those who would pave whatever they can for the sake of a buck.

It's worth stepping back a moment here to put 'de-extinction' in its historical context. Brand and his gang are part of a movement of thinkers who believe that the best way to save the Earth is to rebuild it from the bottom up. The advent of genetic modification, nanotechnology and synthetic biology, they believe, will soon allow them to do this: to take naturally occurring organisms apart and recreate them without any of the pesky glitches that evolution has conferred on them. To start nature again, from scratch, and get it right this time.

This is an intellectual project that goes back to the very beginning of modern Western thought. 'The births of living creatures are ill-shapen, so are all innovations, which are the births of time,' wrote Francis Bacon in 1597. Bacon was quite open, as were many earlier philosophers, about humanity's duty to dominate the rest of life. The most 'noble' aim that anyone could pursue, Bacon wrote in *Novum Organum,* was to 'extend the power and dominion of the human race itself over the universe'.

Not much has changed in four hundred years. Brand's mantra, 'we are as gods and we have to get good at it', is simply a rewording of Bacon's ambition. This is a project that sees the world as imperfect and that sees the duty of enlightened human engineers as correcting the imperfections. The end result will be a planned and controlled world of wealth, happiness and peace for all: a rationalist utopia, designed and run by rationalists. Probably we will be able to live for ever, having worked out how to 'download' our consciousness into machines. Would there be much difference, given that we are machines already?

The de-extinctors are right about one thing: humans have always been engineers, toolmakers, tinkerers. Those characteristics have got us to where we are, for better or for worse. From wheat strains to breeds of dog, humanity has been busy 'improving' on nature since history began. But we are now approaching a point at which our power to do so will move way beyond this kind of slow, gradual tinkering. Soon we will be able to build our own worlds, and there are plenty of people slavering at the prospect.

In April this year, Antony Evans (who hails from – you guessed it – California) sought to raise funds on the crowd-funding website Kickstarter to create, using synthetic biology, 'natural lighting with no electricity' in the form of glowing plants. Evans imagines a future in which trees glow in the streets, replacing street lamps. No longer discrete organisms with their own needs and purpose, trees will become our silent slaves. Evans sought to raise $65,000 for the project; he ended up with nearly $500,000.

Say what you like about religion, but at least it teaches us that we are not gods. The ethic that is promoted by the de-extinctors and their kind tells us that we are gods and we should act like them. While it may sometimes pose as conservation or environmentalism, this is in reality the latest expression of human chauvinism; another manifestation of the empire of *homo sapiens sapiens*. If it marches forward it will usher in the end of the animal, and the end of the wild. It will lead us towards a New Nature, entirely the product of our human-ness. There will be no escape from ourselves. We might call it Total Civilisation.

'I am Stewart Brand, reviver of extinct species,' declaims Brand on the web forum Reddit. I am Ozymandias, king of kings: pleased to meet you.

Sometimes I ask myself why I give a shit about any of this. Why do I feel that the forests matter? The becks, the orang-utans, the hornbills, the giant anteaters, the speckled wood butterflies? I always come back to the same answer: I don't know, and yet I do. I can't quite explain it, but I know that these things stir feelings in me that point towards a greatness that cannot be found within the human world alone. And I know that the possibility of these things disappearing for ever from the world brings about in me a passion, an anger, a fear and a frustration that is primal, atavistic and probably as old as the caves. Because I am an animal and this is my world; my birthright. It is my place. And I know that these things count, whether I can explain it or not.

Those feelings – those passions – are a result of my embodied, intuitive reaction to the world I am part of. They are the result of me being an animal in a world of beauty, depth and complexity, and feeling that this external abundance is a part of my internal life. They are a result of me feeling, assuming, *knowing* that the Earth is not a machine; that all is alive, still. They are a result of me feeling small in the face of all this, and being grateful for the humility this forces on me, even if sometimes it may be against my will.

I could rationalise all this if I needed to. I could tell myself that it is a feeling that has evolved because it is useful to me in my struggle to survive as an organism in the maelstrom of life. I could tell myself, as the biologist E. O. Wilson does in his book *Consilience*, that we stand in awe of nature, or of God, in the same way a dog stands in awe of its master. We are primates, we need leaders and our apparently universal desire to abase ourselves before something greater is simply 'animal submissive behaviour' gone awry.

This, of course, is the kind of thing that scientists say. But it is also the kind of intellectual contortion that my culture demands of me if I am to legitimise the way I experience the world. I was brought up to believe that humans are objective, disinterested observers of a fixed external reality and that we should behave as such. But this point of view is not science; it is ideology. And in any case, as Wilson himself admits, even if it were right, it wouldn't much matter.

Because the fact is, many of us do have these senses; we do see something in the wild world that we need. We do feel awe; we do see something magical or even holy in waterfalls and cloud formations and herds of ibex. These experiences are real, and they are not going away. If we have a sense that there is something higher than our reason can explain to be found in the woods and the fields, and if this is the real reason our hearts break when the woods and the fields are bulldozed in the name of economics, then this sense, like our ability to love or to experience beauty or ugliness, is entirely 'subjective'. But it is also entirely real.

Our culture stands in awe of science, and is repeatedly thrilled by what it can do, and understandably. But it is far less keen to talk about what it can't do. We tend to allow the excitement generated by men in lab coats rebuilding frogs to blind us to the reality of what science is: simply a method of finding out how things work. This is hardly a small thing, but it is not as a great a thing as some of its public advocates would have us believe either. And neither is it, as some are very keen for us to believe, the basis of a new ethic. Aldous Huxley, a keen follower of the science of his time, put it well:

> Reality as actually experienced contains intuitions of value and significance, contains love, beauty, mystical ecstasy, intimations of godhead. Science did not and still does not possess intellectual instruments with which to deal with these aspects of reality. Consequently it ignored them and concentrated its attention upon such aspects of the world as it could deal with . . . in the arts, in philosophy, in religion men are trying – doubtless, without complete success – to describe and explain the non-measurable, purely qualitative aspects of reality.

Science can show us the workings of the universe in ways we could never once have imagined, and it can change our perspective on that universe radically by doing so. But it can't tell us what matters in our human lives, and why, and neither can it tell us why we see what we see, and feel what we feel, and what we should do about any of that. Science might be able to tell us how to resurrect a mammoth, but it can never tell us whether we should.

And so I ask myself again why the recreation of dead creatures offends me so, and I come up with an answer I am not comfortable with. I think I regard what the de-extinctors are planning as some kind of . . . what? Sin? Blasphemy? These are not words I use – I am reluctant even to write them – and yet, what else is this? What else is this recreation of life in the image of a certain type of human being, if it is not in some way unholy?

Perhaps that word – holy – is the key. The Old English word *halig*, remember, has the same root as the word 'whole'. If you see the Earth as whole, entire of itself, interconnected, then you see yourself as part of a wider living thing. If, on the other hand, you see the Earth as a machine and all living things as separate parts, then you have no reason not to tinker with them to your own design. What you will end up with then is men playing with toys, only the toys are living creatures, whole species – eventually a planet. This is Earth-as-playground. And what will your 'valid criticisms' be then?

I wonder if there has been a society in history so uninterested in the sacred as ours; so little concerned with the life of the spirit, so contemptuous of the immeasurable, so dismissive of those who feel that these things are essential to human life. The rationalist vanguard would have us believe that this represents progress: that we are heading for a new Jerusalem, a real one this time, having sloughed off 'superstition'. I am not so sure. I think we are missing something big. Most cultures in human history have maintained, or tried to maintain, some kind of balance between the material and the immaterial; between the temple and the marketplace. Ours is converting the temples into luxury apartments and worshipping in the marketplace instead. We are allergic to learning from the past, but I think we could learn something here.

The rationalist delusion has a strong grip on our culture, and that grip has been getting stronger during my lifetime. Every year, it seems, the areas of life that remain uncolonised by scientific or economic language or assumptions grow fewer. The success that science has had in explaining what can be explained has apparently convinced many people that it can explain everything, or will one day be able to do so. The success that economics has had in monetising the things that science can explain has convinced many that everything of significance can be monetised.

Environmentalists and conservationists are as vulnerable to these literalist trends as anyone else, and many of them have persuaded themselves that, in order to be taken seriously by those with the power to save or destroy, they must speak this language too. But this has been a Faustian bargain. Argue that a forest should be protected because of its economic value as a 'carbon sink', and you have nothing to say when gold or oil of much greater value are discovered beneath it.

Speaking the language of the dominant culture, the culture of human empire that measures everything it sees and demands a return, is not a clever trick but a clever trap. Omit that sense of the sacred in nature – play it down, diminish it, laugh nervously when it is mentioned – and you are lost, and so is the world that moved you to save it for reasons you are never quite able to explain.

I'll say it plainly, because I've worked myself up to it: in nature I see something divine, and when I see it, it moves me to humility, not grandiosity, and that is good for me and good for those I come into contact with. I don't want to be a god, even if I can. I want to be a servant of god, if by god we mean nature, life, the world. I want to be small in the world, belong to it, help it along, protect myself from its storms and try to cause none myself.

I know there are others who feel like this, and I know there are others who don't. It is not a position to be argued from. I don't want to try to convince you if you're not already convinced. If you don't feel it, you don't feel it. I do, and I can't argue it away. There it is.

But here's my suggestion: this feeling is not an awkward and embarrassing stumbling block in the way of a rational assessment of the reality of ecosystems. It is not something to be ashamed of, not something to be dismissed as 'romanticism' or 'religion' – both curse words in the culture we have made. It is something else. It is an old, animal intuition that serves me, and others, well, as it has served humanity for millennia, from the caves at Niaux onwards. And those of us who do feel it – well, we have a duty. We have a duty to talk about it, openly, calmly, incisively, without recourse to pseudo-science or the alienating language of established religions or New Age cults.

Why? Because this sense, that nature is somehow sacred, is widely held, crosses cultural and national boundaries, and is a potentially powerful defence against the intellectual assaults of the New Gods, for whom the world is a workshop and wild nature is a collection of parts to be fitted together in whatever order we fancy. It seems to me that believing, and confidently stating, that nature has some intrinsic, inherent value beyond the instrumental, gives us a reason to stand back from the Temple, not to enter it, to leave it undefiled.

Is this 'irrational'? Very well, then: it is irrational, and it is no less real for that. The de-extinctors would have us believe that we are already gods, already engineers of life, that nature is gone, the wild is dead, the only future is their beloved 'Anthropocene'. But they are wrong. Humans have changed much, and we control much, or try to, but we have never stepped over this threshold before. We have never moved towards the creation of life itself, and the consequent, inevitable elimination of wild nature.

There are two very different ways of looking at a mammoth. In the Black Chamber we see one. In de-extinction we see another. Which way are we going to walk? What are we going to choose? Spiritual teachers throughout history have all taught that the divine is reached through simplicity, humility and self-denial: through the negation of the ego and respect for life. To put it mildly, these are not qualities that our culture encourages. But that doesn't mean they are antiquated; only that we have forgotten why they matter. This is not something we ought to be proud of.

It seems to me that re-cultivating values such as these, rather than building toy mammoths in laboratories, is probably a more serious and useful response to the current crisis of nature. That crisis is at root a crisis of civilisation – a civilisation that has lost sight of any values beyond the quantifiable and the anthropocentric, and is increasingly proud of the fact. At this stage in history, we should at least try to find the words for what is so plainly missing. This is not an indulgence, but a necessity.

I think there is something in the Black Chamber that we still need. Science cannot locate it, and art can only circle it, enquiring. For ten thousand years we have built our own domes in search of it. Now that we have killed God and raised Progress in His place, we only seem to need it more. Yet even the return of God would not take us back to what the Magdalenians saw in the creatures they saved for eternity from the fate of all things that live.

The animals on the walls are the animals in our minds,

and neither have yet faded from view. Stand and look at them long enough and we may begin to grasp what they meant and why they matter. Refuse to look and they will stay asleep, like Arthur's knights under the hill. But unlike Arthur's knights in those old legends, they won't rise up to save us in our hour of need. Nothing will rise but the roots and the tendrils, growing over the remnants of our projects and our wishful thoughts, as they have done so many times before. And the bison and the ibex will still be there, deep in the rock, waiting to be found again.

Dark Mountain, issue 5, 2014

The Old Yoke

Green men they are called; or, less poetically, 'foliate heads'. They captivated me from a young age and I have been collecting them, on and off, for years. I have over a dozen dotted around my house now. I have line drawings, paperweights, even a candlestick with leaves winding their way up the shaft. There is a wooden beam on the ceiling of the room where I work that has eight green men strung along it. Two of them are replicas of stone bosses from the ceiling of Rosslin Chapel in Scotland; another is a wooden copy of a foliate head from the choir stall of Lincoln Cathedral. This year saw my fortieth birthday, and I am toying with the idea of having a green man tattooed on my shoulder to commemorate the occasion.

I don't want to give the impression that I'm obsessed. Obsessions are constant and all-consuming, whereas my interest in the green man is sporadic but ongoing. But whenever I go into an old church, the first thing I look for is a foliate head. It's like a treasure hunt. You may find your treasure hiding among the choir stalls or the bench ends, in the stained-glass windows, in roof bosses or as gargoyles on the guttering. But you will find it, surprisingly often, and when you do it is like finding a golden egg.

What is this thing? Its origins and meaning are obscure and probably now unknowable, which is one of the attractions. Why do we find, carved in old Christian sanctuaries, a strange, even daemonic, very un-Christian symbol?

There are plenty of hypotheses, and they vary depending on who you talk to. The paganistically inclined like to claim that green men are relics of pre-Christian religions that have been incorporated into churches. I have heard, variously, that the green man represents the spirit of the greenwoods, the rebirth of nature, a rebellion against Christianity or a symbol of the constancy of the wild. Everybody who knows the green man has a favourite theory about what he is and why he is there.

Here is mine, which has no more or less basis in fact than any other. It begins nearly a thousand years ago, on the best-known date in English history: 1066.

*

This was the year in which, for the first and the last time, the kingdom of England was comprehensively conquered. The battle of Hastings, in which most of the English ruling class and its fighting men were annihilated, is well known enough not to need any explanation here. King Harold II was killed, and Duke Guillaume of Normandy (later Anglicised to 'William') seized the English crown, despite having no serious claim to it.

If school history classes are anything like they were when I was a boy, the battle of Hastings will be taught in some detail, and its aftermath barely mentioned. But Hastings was the beginning, not the end, of the Norman campaign to conquer England. For the next decade, a widespread guerrilla insurgency was fought across the nation in an attempt to drive the Normans out. It was a grassroots rising with modern parallels in the French resistance to the Nazis or the Viet Cong's stand against the Americans. Few people today know much about it, and until I began researching it three years ago for a novel set in the period, I didn't either. But it has arguably shaped the England we still live in.

After Hastings, Guillaume expected the remnants of the English elite to grant him the crown. Instead, the Witan, or high council, gathered in London and acclaimed a new king: not the duke, but Edgar, the fourteen-year old grandson of a previous English king, Edmund Ironside. Until the Normans introduced the concept of automatic hereditary monarchy to England, kings were elected by the Witan. And this one, even after Hastings, refused to elect Guillaume.

The duke dealt with this problem as he dealt with every other throughout his life: through the use of extreme violence. He marched his army up through the south-east, burning, looting and raping as he went. He circled London, burned Southwark to the ground and then marched west, brutalising the populations of Buckinghamshire, Bedfordshire, Middlesex and Hertfordshire. Soon enough, the Witan caved in. They had no means of resisting what the Normans had brought. On Christmas Day, Guillaume le Bâtard – William the Bastard, as his own people knew him – was crowned King of England at Westminster Abbey.

What did Guillaume expect from England, and what did the English expect from him? It was not the first time a foreign king had seized the English throne; only half a century earlier the Danish king Cnut had been crowned after a similarly successful invasion. Cnut had made changes to the way England was governed, but he hadn't sought, or needed, to hold its people down by force. The Danish king's takeover had been a transition of elites, which had barely affected the mass of people. Perhaps the English thought that, after the most terrifying year in living memory, this latest foreign lord might turn out to be a new Cnut: stern but benign, maybe even their protector.

They were soon to be disabused. The first law enacted by Guillaume, in January 1067, declared that all the land in England now belonged to the crown. All who held land, from the highest lord to the lowest peasant, held it now on sufferance from him. This was a revolution from the top, and it allowed William to pay back the mercenaries who had made up much of his invading force by parcelling out the nation's acres to them. Then he increased taxes, several times (the Domesday Book was a tax collector's manual). Then he appointed his friends, relatives and lieutenants to the highest offices in the land. Within a decade of the conquest, the number of English people in positions of high authority could be counted on the fingers of one hand.

At this point, the fires of rebellion began to burn. The Normans had tied down the south-east of England, but much of the rest of the nation was yet to be won. The sons of the late King Harold, who had fled to Ireland, made sorties into Devon and Cornwall. Edgar, the almost-king, fled into exile in Scotland, where he gained the support of King Malcolm. On the Welsh borders, an outlaw known as Eadric the Wild fought a vicious guerrilla campaign. On the opposite side of the country, in Lincolnshire, a dispossessed landowner named Hereward put up an astounding display of bravado, holding out on the fen isle of Ely with an army for years and slaughtering Normans by the dozen. And all the time, all over the nation, bands of outlaws took to the woods, the marshes and the wastelands, with the tacit support of local populations, emerging to harass, harry and assassinate the occupying forces.

In 1069, matters came to a head. The Earls of Mercia and Northumbria raised armies, joined forces with young Edgar, Malcolm of Scotland and some of the Welsh princes and declared war on Guillaume. The rising of the north, as it became known, was the best chance the English had to repel the new king, but it was a disaster. Guillaume took his mounted knights north, building castles as he went, and destroyed those parts of the army of resistance that hadn't fled on news of his approach. To ensure that there would be no further hiding place for rebels, he then razed everything that lived or stood over a thousand square miles of land between York and Durham – the infamous 'harrying of the north'. Every animal, every house, every field was destroyed. Chroniclers of the time reported that survivors were reduced to selling their children into slavery, or digging up graves and eating the corpses.

*

Those kinds of memories don't easily fade. Orderic Vitalis, the contemporary Anglo-Norman historian, wrote that 'the English groaned aloud for their lost liberty and plotted ceaselessly to find some way of shaking off a yoke that was so intolerable and unaccustomed'. Six hundred years after the conquest, during the English Civil Wars, radicals still drew on the concept of this 'Norman Yoke' to contextualise the oppression meted out by Charles I, descendant of Guillaume. The notion of a free Anglo-Saxon kingdom remained popular with the Victorians. History, like any other academic discipline, has its fashions, and these days, partly in reaction to Victorian bombast, the idea of a Norman Yoke is sniffed at in the academies. Today, like good postcolonialists, we like to talk of integration and migration, not suppression and resistance.

But I wonder. It seems to me that legacies of 1066 remain with us. Take that first law enacted by Guillaume in 1067. In Anglo-Saxon England, the idea that one man – the king – literally owned the entire land base of the nation would have been unthinkable. Today, it remains a legal reality: England is still owned, as a whole, by the Crown. The hereditary monarchy introduced by the Normans remains too, and the French concept known as 'primogeniture' – in which estates are inherited wholesale by the first-born son, rather than parcelled out between children as was more common in Anglo-Saxon England – is still alive as well.

Tie these threads together and follow them, and things become fascinating. Britain is, today, the country with the second most unequal distribution of land on Earth, after Brazil. More than 70 per cent of the land is owned by less than 2 per cent of the population. Much of this is directly traceable to Guillaume, whose twenty-second-great-granddaughter sits today on the English throne.

Then follow the thread further, and ask yourself whether the development of early modern capitalism in England would have been possible without that concentration of land, and therefore of power and wealth. What about the consequent empire? Did the Industrial Revolution begin in England because that funnel of power and money made it possible? Or what about class, which is directly connected to all of those things? We are still one of the most socially and economically stratified countries in Europe. In today's England, the rulers still drink wine and the plebs still drink beer, just as they did in 1066. The peasants still keep their heads down, too, mostly – whatever the wine-drinking class gets up to with their money or their votes.

What would have happened if things had gone the other way on 14 October 1066, on the hill outside Hastings? Who would we be now? What language would we speak, what land would we inhabit, and what world? What would be carved in our churches, and who would those churches hymn? History never answers questions like these, but every generation gets its chance to ask them.

*

All this leads us, in a roundabout fashion, back to the green men. When I was younger I used to love visiting old Norman churches. As a history nerd, I knew the difference between a Romanesque and a Perpendicular window, and could trace the development of an old church by examining the style of its buttresses and the size of the yew trees in the churchyard. I loved the carved doorways, the thick stone columns and the damp, restrained silence.

These days I have a different relationship with Norman churches: I see them as symbols of oppression. The Normans made a point, after they had consolidated their takeover, of tearing down significant English buildings and replacing them with Norman equivalents. Saxon churches, often made of wood, were replaced with these heavy, squat monuments in eternal stone. A Norman church, to me now, is the equivalent of a motte-and-bailey castle: not simply an interesting old building, but the mark of a conqueror spitting in the face of the conquered.

Perhaps this was how they were seen by the English at the time. The Normans called the guerrilla movement that resisted them after 1066 the 'silvatici' – the men of the woods. The English, it is said, called them the same thing in their own language: green men. In that greenwood rebellion against unwanted masters, we perhaps see the origins of the Robin Hood legend – and of those carvings in the old churches. What would you do if you were an English stonemason in the 1070s, required to help construct an alien church by new masters you despised? How would you show your loathing of them without attracting a penalty? Perhaps you would carve the face of a green man inside the church: perhaps you would bring the spirit of the silvatici into the temple of the enemy. It could be that what adorns the roof beam of my room is not a wistful old nature spirit, but a symbol of resistance to the crushing of a people.

Aeon, 2012

The Bay

I live in a small market town in Cumbria, in northern England. The town sits in a low agricultural bowl, surrounded by rivers that rise from the surrounding hills and flow under, through and around the town and out to the sea. Five miles to the north are the Lake District fells, the only serious mountain range in England. Less than two miles to the south is Morecambe Bay.

Before I moved here, I had no real awareness of the Bay. I knew that Morecambe was a seaside town, but I'd never been there. I heard on the news a few years back about the deaths of a group of Chinese cockle pickers here – they had drowned on the incoming tide – and that seemed grim and strange. But I didn't know how big and curious and captivating a place the Bay was.

I am, slowly, beginning to get it. I am beginning to see that this Bay is a great entity in itself, a living system; not just a backdrop to human activities but a parallel world. This is the largest continual intertidal area in Britain; more than three hundred square kilometres of shifting mud and sand, river estuaries, saltmarshes and sea life. The weather can change its character in minutes, and the position of the sun, the time of year, alters its look and feel. But the sea, above all, sets the mood. High tide down at Bardsea brings the waters almost to the edge of the sea road, with only a barrier of silted rushes between solid land and salt water. But at low tide, everything changes. At low tide Morecambe Bay becomes liminal space, a universe entire of itself.

I spend as much time down here as I can, writing and walking. Last summer, when I was writing a book, I used my need for writerly solitude as an excuse to drive my old camper van down to the edge of the Bay, leave the doors open and write. And when writing had taken me over for too long and I needed to ground myself again, I ran. I changed my clothes and struck off out to sea and I ran as far as I could from land, across the shifting sands, out into the middle of the Bay. This can be dangerous if you don't know the tide times or you don't know what quicksand looks like, but its dangers are also overstated, or at least that's what I told myself. I liked this, anyway, because it meant that nobody else would ever follow me. It meant I was alone with the sand and the sky.

On the first day of September last year I wrote until midday and then I ran. I ran straight out, heading south-west. The sun was high and the sky was empty of clouds and the sea was a silver line on the horizon. I ran towards the great black rectangular block of Heysham nuclear power station, ten miles distant on the far shore. I ran for fifteen minutes and stopped at a shallow, silver river, exposed only when the tide is out, which was flowing low and snakelike across the sand. I had never seen it before. I turned.

Behind me was the far shore, my van a white speck on it, the hills rising behind it, the Coniston fells clear in the distance, their bands and steps clean in the white light. Along to the south the coast ran down to the old industrial town of Barrow, the ruined castle on Piel Island just visible, an intimidation of distant wind turbines out to sea. On the far shore the tabletop of Ingleborough was clear on the horizon, the townlets of the Morecambe shore stretched out in silver, Blackpool tower a thin needle in the late summer haze.

I wasn't alone there, though I was the only human. On the water a great flock of gulls was bobbing, moving on the slow current, sometimes taking off in pairs or singly, circling, coming down again. They were cawing and curling and calling in the sun. I crouched down and began sifting the muddy sand through my fingers. Tiny crustaceans skipped and crawled through the water. I looked up as a gull careened overhead, screaming.

And I had the strangest feeling, then. I felt as if I was part of something very much bigger than myself. I didn't think it, I felt it, and the feeling came entirely unbidden. I felt this place, this edgeland, this world of wing and water – I felt how it was working. I felt the clockwork of it, the movement, felt the blood of it flowing in the salt sea and in the movement of the gulls and in the sand and the riverflow. This was all part of some great living engine, working a task, ticking over, each of its constituent parts performing their function. I was looking on but I had no role. I wasn't wanted here, or unwanted. I was jetsam, passing by on the tide.

*

In his essay *The Etiquette of Freedom*, the poet Gary Snyder makes a distinction between 'natural' and 'wild'. He uses the word 'nature', he explains, in its broadest sense, to mean 'the physical universe and all its properties'. In this sense, everything on Earth is 'natural' because it doesn't break the laws of nature. A rainforest is natural, but so is a space rocket. A badger is natural, but so is a plastic bag.

The word 'wild', on the other hand, denotes those portions of the physical universe that remain free from the agency of humanity; which are as yet untamed by the predator Man. Snyder writes that this definition of wildness comes

> very close to being how the Chinese defined the term Dao, the way of Great Nature: eluding analysis, beyond categories, self organising, self informing, playful, surprising, impermanent, insubstantial, independent, complete, orderly, unmediated, freely manifesting, self authenticating, self willed, complex, quite simple.

The undomesticated animal; the self-propagating plant; the unturned soil; the unmanaged woodland: these, says Snyder, are 'wild'. In this sense, the Bay is wild. Perhaps it is the wildest place in England, assuming that it is in England. Assuming that it is within the territory of Man and not the territory of the birds and the razor shells and the curling blades of kelp and the grey-brown waters.

We would like to think so, because we would like to imagine that the Bay can be tamed, as we imagine that everything wild can be tamed, should we choose. We would like to imagine this because we suspect, on some level, that it cannot. In 2004, twenty-three Chinese immigrant workers, who spoke little English and had misunderstood the tide times, were drowned harvesting the Bay's cockle beds. There was some national outrage at this. It seemed incongruous; here we were in the mechanised, mediated twenty-first century, and poor cockle pickers were still drowning on English mudflats, as they have done for millennia.

A lot of lessons were drawn from that tragedy; lessons about immigration and illegality and gangmasters and cheap labour and what our culture is prepared to pay for and turn a blind eye to. But the wider lesson was that the wild is still with us and needs to be negotiated with and respected. The Bay has been drowning humans since there were humans, and if you stand on the shore and watch the tide come in, you can see why. The seabed is shallow for a long distance out from the shore, and the angle of the sands is so obtuse that when the tide comes in it approaches like a mini-tsunami.

On the stone pier in the Bayside village of Arnside earlier this year, I watched the bore rising, heralded by a long series of blasts on a siren, which echoed around the Bay as if warning of an air raid. Within minutes, a white line of water had built up across the horizon. Then it was breaking on the ramps and the bridge struts, and rising up the mudflats unstoppably. It could not have been outrun. If you don't know what you're doing or where you are, or if you're not paying attention or you have had a close encounter with its many pools of shimmering quicksand, the Bay can claim you, more quickly than you would have believed possible.

Not that this happens very often any more. Before the Furness Railway was built around its perimeter in the 1850s, it was a different matter. For much of the history of human habitation around the Bay, getting from the Lancashire shore to the Furness peninsula meant crossing the sands. It was easier than attempting to walk or take pack-horses or carts across the saltmarshes around the edges or the hills and fells of Cumberland to the north. The old paths across the Bay still exist, and so does the Queen's Guide to the Sands, the only such position in England, created after locals petitioned the king in the early sixteenth century in an attempt to alleviate the many drownings that resulted from people trying to cross the Bay by themselves or with dubious local guides. The position is unpaid but it does come with a free house owned by the Crown. Nobody takes packhorses across the dangerous, shifting paths of the Bay any more, but the current Guide, Cedric Robinson, a former fisherman who was appointed in 1963, leads regular charity walks across the Bay by way of compensation.

Before the Queen's Guides, the monks of Cartmel Priory would escort travellers across the Bay, for an appropriately holy fee. The Priory was dissolved by Henry VIII, and four of its monks were hanged for resisting the tide of history. The remaining buildings of the priory are a tourist attraction today, but other built relics scattered around the Bay have not been blessed with tea shops and introductory leaflets: the old canal at Ulverston, at just a mile long said to be the shortest in the country, which carried goods ships from the Bay to the town for just a decade before the railways came and knocked it into the crumbling, appealing historical void in which remains today; the great shipyards at Barrow, which furnished the Empire; the long-gone ironworks at Carnforth (and its long-gone railway station refreshment room, in which much of David Lean's *Brief Encounter* was filmed in 1945; in a burst of enthusiasm, the refreshment room was recently recreated in its original form, and now draws film buffs from across the world).

And, beneath the waves, or sometimes half above them, the dozens of wrecks of ships that have found the tides and the sands here too much to handle over the centuries. Sometimes, running across the sands at low tide, I see their ghosts: a few wooden ribs rising from the mudflats, rusted plates of riveted steel merging with the sand. The barnacles make good use of them, the Bay absorbs them, the engine keeps turning.

Relics are more easily created than we like to think. Walk around the Bay today and you can see tomorrow's relics already in the process of being created. You can also see that the strange juxtaposition of the wildness of the sands and the human industry of the fringes continues as it has for centuries. Beyond the reclaimed saltmarshes, where there were once ironworks, steelworks, shipyards or docks, there are now windfarms, nuclear power stations, the Glaxo pharmaceutical plant at Ulverston – soon to be rebuilt and expanded – and, in Barrow, where the Furness peninsula slopes off into the sea, the great, sinister hulking sheds of BAE Systems, where Britain's dwindling nuclear submarine fleet is constructed and maintained.

The 'energy coast' they are calling it now, the west side of the Bay and the west coast of Cumbria. The arms firm BAE and the Sellafield nuclear power plant are the big employers around here, joined more recently by the up-and-comers, wind energy in particular. Stand on the dunes at Walney Island off Barrow and look out to sea, and the horizon is filled by wind turbines bigger, and in greater number, than you thought wind turbines could ever be. Never mind the cosy green fantasies about 'human-scale' renewable energy: this is the future and, like the past, it is breathtakingly vast in its ambition and its engineering. Walney is currently the world's largest offshore windfarm. Maybe it will bring tourists as well as electricity. Maybe it will save us; and how we need to believe that.

But none of this has really tamed the Bay. All of this human energy happens around its fringes, and although parts of the shore have been reclaimed from the sea and turned over to the farmers, the expanse of sand and wind and water remains wild still. Not that people don't try to put their stamp on it. For a century or so there has been talk about building a bridge across the Bay, from Heysham or Morecambe to Barrow. At around twelve miles long, the Morecambe Bay Bridge, if it ever got off the drawing board, would be one of the longest in the world. As Barrow's economy continues to slide, demands for its construction, with all the usual attached promises of job creation and 'regeneration', have grown louder, though not loud enough to give the local Build Duddon and Morecambe Bridges Party more than 400 votes at the last general election. In line with the times, the latest proposal is for a bridge lined with wind turbines, which would also act as a tidal barrage, drawing energy from the Bay. If such a beast were ever built, it would change, perhaps destroy, the character of the Bay for ever. The advocates of 'sustainability', with a rich irony, would have succeeded where the old extractive industries failed.

Between the estuaries of the rivers Kent and Leven, protruding from the north of the Bay like a crooked finger, is Humphrey Head, a slightly otherworldly limestone outcrop, which features the only cliffs on this coast. Climb up Humphrey Head on a winter or spring day and walk across its limestone pavements, between the storm-bent trees. The place has quite a different feel to the low sand shores that make up most of the Bay. At the foot of the cliffs here is a trickle of water: all that remains of a once holy well. People once walked here from across the north of England to take the water, which was said to have therapeutic properties. Button-backed miners would come all the way from the Durham pits, bringing their hope with them.

There is a story about Humphrey Head, though it is a story that is told about many other places too. The story is that here, in the 1390s, the last wolf in England was killed by a contingent of local men, who pursued it with pikes and trapped it in the limestone bluffs. I choose to believe this, because the story fits the place so well, and because it suits me to think that the elimination of one of the last great mammals in Britain, the severing of one of our links with our own wild past, at least happened in a place – a rare place now – where wildness still means something.

There are no wolves today, and nobody drinks from the well, but there is something both wild and therapeutic about Humphrey Head still. On a clear day, standing on the limestone pavement, you can see the Bay laid out before you like a map. But it's better when the sun has gone and the clag has descended as if the past has returned. On a misty day you can be here again with the last of the wolves while the gulls circle around you, dimming in and out of the clouds like spectres, and the oystercatchers pipe under the cliffs and the sands continue to shift and the waters flow from the holy well, and the untameable Bay goes on around you, its great engine turning over still with the years and the tides.

The Clearing, 2013

Rescuing the English

Some years back, I was driving through northern England with a friend. On a Cumbrian A-road west of Kendal, we passed a lay-by in which was situated a typical British roadside snack bar: a white caravan, a couple of plastic garden chairs, pink and yellow Day-Glo cardboard stars advertising chips and fried breakfasts and tea. The full English.

On top of this caravan was an aerial, and attached to the aerial, blowing in the wind that was coming off Morecambe Bay, was a George Cross, the English national flag – a common sight now across the nation, though I'm sure it never used to be when I was young.

'What do you think that's about?' my friend asked. 'Why do you think you see so many of them in places like this now?'

I said I hadn't thought about it. But it seemed my friend had. He told me it reminded him of a road trip he had taken when he was younger across the southern states of the US: the former Confederacy. There, he said, you would often see the old Confederate flag flying in similar places: unofficial, at once underground and open, an act of defiance.

'It's not the same,' he said, 'but it's sort of similar, isn't it? It's like the sign of a people that lost. But they're saying, "We're still here."'

We're still here. I think of this now when I see UKIP's rise in the polls, or I read that levels of both immigration and objections to immigration are at record highs, or that trust in the political system continues to collapse, or that the euro is on the brink again, or that 45 per cent of Scottish voters want to break away from the UK. I think of this and I wonder about England. I wonder about the future of this great national elephant, shifting its bulk in the peeling glamour of the British imperial room. I wonder what England is, and where it is going and what its people want to be. I wonder if it will survive as a nation, and whether it matters, and I wonder what will happen next.

*

Seven years ago, I published a book called *Real England*. It was both a personal state-of-the-nation report and a record of my own anxieties. For years I'd sensed an ongoing, hard–to-pin-down loss of many of the things I felt made my country distinctive. I'd watched local pubs being turned into theme bars or pricey flats. The old town-centre breweries were going with them, and the collapse of independent shops was transforming high streets into identical colonnades of brand names. In the countryside, what little that remained of a particularly English rural culture was being emptied out, as villages became commuter dormitories or dead collectives of second homes for the wealthy. In the cities, independent shops and pubs and markets and clubs were being gentrified out of existence, and more sinister things were happening, too: public streets and open spaces were being privatised, enclosed and policed by private security guards. The small and the local, the traditional and the distinctive, were being stamped out by the powerful, the placeless and the very, very profitable.

This was not a phenomenon confined to England. Around the world, an increasingly deregulated consumer capitalism was, and is, elbowing aside local cultures and national identities and, in many cases, democracy as well. Everyone in politics and the media seemed to agree on how wonderful this all was, and all the official figures from the World Bank and the OECD and the ranks of chief economists and chancellors proved that we were all better off. It was to be Tiger Economies and the Global Race and Economic Growth for ever. The world was now a giant airport lounge through which happy consumers could wander at will, picking baubles off the shelf, unmoored from history, place and meaning. Concerns about any of this were usually dismissed as 'nostalgia': a harmless but irrelevant longing for a 'rose-tinted past'.

I must have spent about nine months wandering England researching that book, talking to lock keepers and farmers and canal boaters, café owners and MPs and market traders, landlords and apple growers and campaigners against second homes. Above and beyond all of their specific grievances, I sensed a strange unease. It wasn't about particular local problems, and though it was sometimes voiced, more often it was unspoken. I hadn't expected it, but it was definitely there. Many people seemed to feel unacknowledged, unlistened to, ignored, looked down on: not just as individuals, but as a people, as a nation. As the English.

The United Kingdom is, depending on your politics, either a state made up of four nations or a state made up of three and a half. Either way, England is by far the biggest, with around 85 per cent of the British population, and its size has traditionally made it the dominant voice in the relationship. The British Empire was not an exclusively English project (whatever Celtic nationalists might like to suggest) but it certainly caused a specific register of Englishness – southern, bourgeois, mercantile, expansionist – to become associated with Britain as a whole, and the Victorian establishment's worldview was imbued with a strong sense of a manifest Anglo-Saxon destiny.

The collapse of this brand of imperial Englishness marched in step with the collapse of the empire that had created it. Then, as part of the reaction to that empire, an academic and intellectual effort began in the second half of the twentieth century to 'deconstruct' the English national identity, and with it the very concept of nations. Waves of immigration from the former empire after World War Two began to change the nature of the English population, forcing a reconsideration of what identity meant and who belonged where.

By the beginning of this century, it seemed that Englishness was an identity in official retreat. The contrast with attitudes a century earlier was revealing. The political and cultural establishments no longer talked about an Anglo-Saxon destiny. Rather they talked about a 'multicultural Britain' in which the English were just one culture among many. In this narrative, the English were a nation of 'mongrels', who had been 'multicultural' right from the start. The word 'English' should rightly appear in inverted commas, in fact, to emphasise its 'problematic' nature. Even the English flag was recast as a symbol of racism and bigotry, despite the fact that most of the tiny far-right groupings in Britain were actually waving the same flag as all the mainstream political parties – the Union Jack.

Constitutionally, the United Kingdom was reconstructed

in the late 1990s: Scotland was given its parliament, Wales its assembly and Northern Ireland its peace process. England remained the only UK nation to which power was not devolved, and whose people were not consulted about their governance. English governance, in fact, was a mess, but nobody wanted to talk about it. Scottish, Welsh and Northern Irish MPs were voting on laws that applied only to England, while English MPs were left out of decisions being made about other UK nations. Those other nations were receiving more money per head from the UK Treasury, despite the fact that most of the poorest parts of Britain were in England.

Meanwhile, the political establishment at Westminster, increasingly desperate to keep the kingdom united, began playing up the notion of 'Britishness' as a unitary identity. The Labour governments of 1997 to 2010 were notorious for their refusal to acknowledge the English polity. Scottish Prime Minister Gordon Brown even became the focus of an online campaign called 'Say England', demanding that he spoke the name of the nation he was governing, something he seemed oddly reluctant to do unless the World Cup was on. Brown preferred to refer instead, as his protégé Ed Miliband still does, to 'the nations and regions of Britain' – the nations being Scotland, Wales and Northern Ireland, and the regions being the administrative chunks into which Labour had divided England in 1998. England, it seemed, was no longer a nation even in the eyes of its own government.

Then, of course, there was immigration. Since the late 1990s, migration into the UK had risen to historically unprecedented levels. In the last recorded year, ending June 2014, over 580,000 new people arrived in Britain – to put that in context, it is ten times as many as arrived in 1985 –

and the great majority had settled in England, where over 90 per cent of Britain's ethnic-minority population lives. The 2011 census revealed the scale of change. Thirteen per cent of England's population was now foreign-born, and in four English cities, including the capital, English people had become an ethnic minority. The population had risen by 4 million in a decade, with two-thirds of this growth caused by immigration, and the rate of movement showed no sign of slowing down.

England was changing fast, and growing numbers of its people were beginning to feel unmoored and unspoken for. What England was and would become, what it meant to be English in the twenty-first century, and who decided, were increasingly anxious questions, but nobody would acknowledge them through the official channels. Meanwhile, the pressure on schools, hospitals, housing and infrastructure caused by the rapid population increase was having a real-world impact, especially on working-class and lower middle-class English people, who were bearing the brunt of the pressure created by the influx of newcomers while reaping few or none of the benefits.

This was the state of England in the early twenty-first century. From a position of global dominance and cultural complacency a century before, it was now a nation in the midst of an identity crisis. So what did Englishness mean? And how could that question be explored in an intellectual environment in which English identity was caricatured as either nostalgic or nasty?

Today, these questions seem easier to ask. That sense of unhappiness that I noticed nearly a decade ago is finding a voice. Politically, the combination of a coalition government, a rolling economic crisis, the Scottish referendum and the rise of UKIP is making a continued denial of Englishness and a promotion of a unitary Britishness increasingly untenable. Culturally, too, something seems to be changing. Opinion polls show increasing numbers of people, from all backgrounds and ethnicities, identifying themselves as 'English' rather than 'British'. From folk music to food, from fiction to TV drama, there is a tentative sense of a renewed cultural Englishness beginning to creep into the light.

We're still here, say the flags. There are more of them every year, and they seem the most visible aspect of that coalescing English voice, one that hasn't been heard for a long time, but that is growing in volume. What that voice will end up saying is now the big question.

*

A nation is a story that a people chooses to tell about itself, and at its heart is a stumbling but deep-felt need for those people to be connected to the place they live and to each other. Humans in all times and places have needed ancestors, history, a place to be and a sense of who they are as a collective, and modernity and rationalism have not abolished these needs. They are needs that stimulate great passions, which in turn can do great harm, as history has shown time and again, but they are unlikely ever to go away.

A nation, in other words, is about belonging – to a specific place that is not quite like another place, and to a collective of people you share things with. This kind of belonging can be stifling or liberating, and sometimes both at once, but at its best it gives us a mooring in space and time, without which we are liable to be washed away. If we want to see what a world without belonging would look like, we have only to look around. If an identity is an alliance between people and places, then airport-lounge modernity means taking the places out of the picture. All that is left is people who could be anywhere: citizens of nowhere, consumers of objects and experiences, connected by their little screens, the same white light shining into their faces from Doncaster to Dubai.

In this context, when I think about why I call myself 'English' rather than 'British' – and I always do, from habit and instinct more than from any need to make a statement – it is the places I think about. The small places, especially. I think about osiers by the upper Thames, wind-bent thorns on Dartmoor, millstone grit outcrops in Calderdale. I think about the lanes and the stone rows and the lock cottages and the pub signs. I think about the names: the harrows and hams and tons, the becks and rills and brooks. Wayland's Smithy, Grimsditch, Offa's Dyke, Long Meg. I have always associated England with small, secret things, and Britain with big, bombastic ones. Britain to me is empire and royalty, Satanic mills and the White Man's Burden. England is the still pool under the willows where nobody will find you all day, and the only sound is the fish jumping in the dappled light. It's a romantic vision, I know, but then nations are, like people, at least partly romantic things.

Romance will get you only so far, however. Today, the real England sometimes feels like 50 million people driving around a motorway for ever. The march of the shopping malls, green-belt housing estates and pointy glass skyscrapers continues apace, and the future offers an epic round of building: hundreds of thousands of new houses every year, new airports, new motorways and roads and high-speed rail lines ad infinitum. The population is expected to exceed 70 million within fifteen years, all in the name of growth and with no end in sight. Global capitalism is eating the soul of the nation. What will be left after it has digested its meal?

It is in this context that the current immigration debate can perhaps best be seen. Large-scale immigration is not, as some of its more foaming opponents believe, a conspiracy by metropolitan liberals to destroy English identity. It is a simple commercial calculation. It may cause overcrowding and cultural tension; it may be economically traumatic for some people, and it may drain poorer countries of their own talent, but it is undoubtedly good for growth, which is why 'business leaders' consistently call for more of it. Immigrants are easier to exploit and underpay, and often prepared to work harder and accept fewer rights. If you believe, as our politicians apparently do, that what's good for business is good for everyone, and that a nation is little more than a machine for competing in a 'global race', then mass immigration is an entirely sensible proposition.

The problems that proposition causes are real, and those who support it can no longer get away with shouting 'racist' at the majority who don't. The people of any nation will always want the right to control their own borders and decide on the direction of their culture, and England is no exception. But that majority has its own questions to answer, too. In a nation whose population is ageing, and whose people consistently demand more and cheaper stuff, who is going to do the heavy lifting? If you want a cheap nanny and your cut-price supermarket vegetables picked in all weathers for the minimum wage, then someone has to do it. There is no doubt that large-scale immigration changes the shape, texture and potentially the identity of a nation, but so do out-of-town retail parks, coffee chains, theme pubs, second homes, gentrified cities and privatised streets. If you don't want the population movement, you don't get the cheap, easy consumer lifestyle it facilitates. Which will you choose?

Sometimes, when I look at history, I think that identity is the root of all evil. Sometimes, when I look at the present, I think that we will be lost without it. Perhaps both are true, but it doesn't look like the need for it is going away any time soon. It seems to be a foundation of what it means to be human: a deep, old need. And I keep coming back to England, though I never quite know why.

*

The word 'England' derives from the Old English 'Engla Lond' – land of the Angles. The Angles, along with the Saxons and the Jutes, were one of three Germanic tribes said to have arrived on the shores of post-Roman Britannia in the sixth century, and who would later become known, to distinguish them from the Old Saxons of Germania, as the Anglo-Saxons.

In keeping with the contemporary trend for deconstructing all things English, the Anglo-Saxons have been out of fashion in recent decades, but Engla Lond, or Angland, is the foundation stone on which contemporary England is built. Today, a millennium away from the world of the Anglo-Saxons, we still speak a language derived mostly from the Old English they spoke, and many features of contemporary England, from the monarchy, the Church and the county boundaries right down to field patterns, place names and routes of major roads, have their origins in the age of Bede and Beowulf.

Today, when English history is taught in schools, it often starts in 1066, the only date from school history lessons that most of us can reliably remember. Yet the conquest of England in that year by Viking descendants from Normandy, under the leadership of the brutal Guillaume le Bâtard – William the Bastard, who unsurprisingly preferred to be known as William the Conqueror – resulted in mass dispossession, forced marriage, wide-scale land theft, military rule and the slaughter of those who resisted. Within a few short years, the English elite had been almost entirely replaced by cronies of the new Norman king, and England found itself ruled by a foreign aristocracy who often evinced contempt for Anglo-Saxon culture. It would be another three hundred years before the kings of England again spoke English as their first language.

In other words, the date at which English history is often said to begin is actually the date at which England was colonised. The history of England, seen through the eyes of the ordinary English woman or man, is often a history of dispossession. A case could be made, in fact, that the English were the first victims of the British Empire: without their conquest, that empire could not have been built. The country that invented capitalism and the first modern empire did so on the backs of most of its population. A nation is a story, but there are many different ways to tell it.

If you want to hear that population speak, you have only to listen to an English folk song. Listen to enough of them, and you begin to realise how many are laments. Laments for sons or lovers taken away by the press gang or forced to take the king's shilling. The laments of women waiting seven years for their lovers to return from the sea. The laments of the landless poor. The laments of those hanged or transported for stealing a sheep or a loaf of bread. The laments of those forced into the factories, working for a pittance with no chance of escape. The laments of the bridge builders and the sappers and the miners.

England's tragedy was that its identity became so closely entwined with the commercial and imperial adventures of its elite that it became hard to tell them apart. The smallness of England was replaced with the bombast of Britain, and when Britain's empire collapsed, so did England's sense of itself. Now, as the nation is bought up by a global plutocracy and sold back to its people, questions offer themselves up: can we remember that other history? Does it still matter? In an age in which imperial adventures have been rebranded as 'global competition', can England make itself small again?

*

Britain's forthcoming general election will be a curious affair. It will be fought between three big political parties, all of whom will be loudly committed to the United Kingdom but whose political writ, should they win, will run mainly in England alone. The insurgent populist party, which even has 'UK' in its name, will bang the drum for the union with equal bombast, whilst focusing on an issue – immigration – that affects mainly England.

At times like these, a nation needs its radicals. Unfortunately, the English left is uncomfortable with the idea of nations in general and the English nation in particular. For a long time now, it has been common in leftish circles to argue that nations are dangerous things, that connection to place and history are foreshadows of the twin bogeymen of fascism and racism, and that the future lies with a kind of internationalist humanitarianism, in which such 'parochial' concerns are left behind. The failure of this bloodlessly intellectual vision to capture the human imagination for over a century has still not killed it off.

The English left famously exhibits a strange national self-loathing that doesn't seem mirrored in any comparable European country. Radicals in France, Spain or Greece seem to have no problem couching their challenges to existing authority in language that grasps the meaning of nationhood, and even exhibits pride in it. But in England it is standard for people who consider themselves in some way 'anti-establishment' to sneer at their national identity. This is not a new phenomenon. 'England is perhaps the only great country whose intellectuals are ashamed of their own nationality,' wrote George Orwell in his 1941 pamphlet *The Lion and the Unicorn*. 'In left-wing circles it is always felt that there is something slightly disgraceful in being an Englishman and that it is a duty to snigger at every English institution, from horse racing to suet puddings.'

Whatever the origins of this pathology, the English left should understand that if you're going to take a people's story away from them, you need a better one to replace it with. Attacking that story as the 'parochial' offerings of a 'little Englander' is not going to help your cause. Quite the opposite: this tendency to dismiss or condemn feelings of attachment to place, nation and identity simply means that those things become associated instead with the political right, and when people feel those things are threatened, it will be the right they turn to. This goes a long way to explaining the rise of UKIP. The left's response to that rise – to mock its supporters or call them fascists, or both – shows that at least some of Orwell's England is still with us.

Sometimes, the best way of telling new stories is to reclaim old words. The word 'parochial' might be a good place to start. 'All great civilisations are built on parochialism,' wrote the Irish poet Patrick Kavanagh in 1952. 'Parochialism is universal; it deals with the fundamentals.' Parochialism is universal: it sounds like a contradiction, but only if you don't fully grasp its meaning. 'Parochial' literally means 'of the parish'. It denotes the small and the particular and the specific. It means knowing where you are. It can also mean insular and narrow-minded, but it doesn't have to, any more than 'cosmopolitan' has to mean snobbish and rootless.

This negative meaning has attached itself to the word because contemporary globalised culture is resolutely antiparochial. It sets out to destroy local particularity and our attachment to it, because if we remain attached to it we may not buy into the placeless nowhere civilisation that is being built around the globe in the name of money. At its best, a radical parochialism may be the most effective means of resisting this global machine. As Kavanagh implied, without a parochial culture, there can be no culture at all.

The same is true of the phrase 'little Englander', originally a nineteenth-century term of abuse directed at those who resisted the expansion of empire. A 'Little Englander' was someone who wanted England's influence to stop at its own borders, rather than the nation throwing its weight around in the world. In that sense, a little England sounds pretty good to me. An England that pays attention to its places rather than wiping them out in the name of growth; an England that doesn't have imperial designs; an England that doesn't want to follow America into idiotic wars for the sake of prestige. An England that stops trying to 'punch above its weight', and instead asks why it is punching at all.

If nations are stories, England has a good one to tell: a long and fascinating one, with a balance of darkness and light. It's a story that everyone becomes part of simply by being in England. The Scottish independence campaign last year did a good job of building a civic Scottish identity that people could feel part of whether or not they were ethnically Scottish. In England, which is far more ethnically diverse, it may appear harder to do this, yet the way to do it seems straightforward: just tell the story of England. Tell it from the beginning to the present day, and you will find that everyone in the country has been included in it, wherever they came from and whatever their background.

Is it possible to be a nation without nationalism? To be comfortable with your identity and history without withdrawing into them? To welcome outsiders without forgetting what you are welcoming them to? Englishness, whatever it means, is ever-changing: England today would be largely unrecognisable to someone from 1066, or even 1866. A nation is a process, not a fixed thing, but it has continuities nonetheless. It may be a story, but it is not fiction.

When I think about these questions, I always find myself coming back to the place itself: the woods, the fields, the streets, the towns, the beaches. We live in an age of climate change and mass extinction, burgeoning cities, deepening immersion in technologies of distraction, the spreading ideology of mass consumption. The antidote to this global distancing of humanity from the rest of nature is the slow, messy business of getting to know a landscape. If a nation is a relationship between people and place, then a cultural identity that comes from a careful relationship with that place might be a new story worth telling.

Is there a future, I wonder, in a kind of ecological Englishness – an identity that sees everyone in England as part of its landscapes and thus its history, and that has us all paying closer attention to them: nurturing them instead of concreting them over in the name of the future, or driving past on the way to somewhere else? Could this help build an identity to compete with, and perhaps replace, both the tired pomp of establishment Britain and the deconstructed coldness of the internationalist left? Could that old, smaller England come out from behind the shadow of Britain once more?

It's probably another romantic dream. But nations, like people, need to dream sometimes.

Guardian, 2015

The Witness

The greatest ecological crisis in the Earth's history began with the emission of climate-changing gases by an organism that had spread widely across the planet, colonising many of its ecological niches. These gases – the waste products of its lifestyle – gradually accumulated in the atmosphere. For a long time nothing noticeably changed, but at some stage a tipping point was reached and the planet's climate flipped rapidly from one state to another. The composition of the atmosphere changed, becoming poisonous to most life on Earth, and the planet's mean temperature plunged, precipitating a global ice age. The resulting mass extinction killed perhaps 90 per cent of all living things on Earth.

This was 2.3 billion years ago. The climate-changing organisms were bacteria, and the poisonous gas they emitted was oxygen. Without the planetary catastrophe they precipitated, you, and almost everything you know about the Earth you are part of, would never have come about at all.

All told, there have so far been at least five, and perhaps as many as twenty, 'mass-extinction events' in the history of Earth. This first – known as the 'great oxygen catastrophe' – was the most far-reaching. The last, 66 million years ago, is the one we know best, because it is the most appealing to the human imagination: it wiped out the dinosaurs. Overall, it is estimated that around 98 per cent of all organisms that have ever existed are now gone for ever.

That all created things perish is one of the key teachings of Buddhism. Whatever is subject to origination is subject to cessation. This, it turns out, is true of an individual, a species, an ecosystem or a planetary epoch. Whatever the Buddha saw under the bodhi tree – whatever it was that showed him the ceaselessly changing nature of all things, and convinced him of the misery caused by attempting to cling to temporary states of apparent stability – has been more than borne out by consequent studies of the Earth's geology, ecology and biology. The nature of this Earth is change. The nature of this Earth is endings. The nature of this Earth is extinction.

*

As you read this, the Earth is currently experiencing the latest extinction event in its 4.6-billion-year history. This one, known as the Holocene Extinction, is caused not by cyanobacteria or asteroid impacts, but by human beings. Arguably, it has been going on for at least ten thousand years, since the extinctions of the great megafauna – the mammoths, the ground sloths, the sabre-toothed cats – which in all likelihood were pushed over the brink by human hunters. But it has accelerated greatly since the Industrial Revolution, and gone into overdrive in the last half-century. The current extinction rate is estimated at anything between a hundred and ten thousand times the expected rate of 'background extinction', and as the expansion of the human economy continues, with its associated resource extraction, soil depletion, fossil-fuel combustion, human population increase and mass destruction of ecosystems, the Holocene Extinction is accelerating beyond our ability even to measure it accurately, let alone put any kind of brake on its progress.

What does this mean for us as individuals? If it is our generation's burden to live through this latest collapse in global ecological diversity, the knowledge that we are all complicit increases that burden. Simply being human at this time in history – and particularly being a middle-class human in one of the world's richer nations – makes you, and me, agents of extinction. Much of the Earth's natural wealth and beauty is disappearing, as our species treats the planet like a giant quarry or factory floor. The Earth's climate is changing once again. Tipping points are being reached. Much of nature as we know it is dying away in order that we might have access to smartphones, takeaway coffee, private cars, aeroplane flights and Facebook.

For nearly two decades, starting in the early 1990s, I was involved in environmental activism. That is to say I worked, as did many others, to try to fend off the worst of the damage that humans are doing to the rest of life on Earth. Some of the campaigns I was involved in were successful, and others weren't: this was always a hard battle, and mostly a losing one. But, as time went on, the losing seemed to deepen. It became clear that green campaigners were being overwhelmed on all fronts. Such was the size and the momentum of the human economy, such was its need for growth simply to keep itself functioning, such was the level of denial and demand among most human beings – who, despite our qualms (if we had any) would probably not have sacrificed most of the baubles and benefits that the economic machine was giving us – that the chances of preventing the Holocene Extinction from rolling onward came to seem essentially non-existent.

Environmental campaigning, like any form of politics, is predicated on control. It is about preventing negative things from happening and trying to channel society towards what you regard as more positive values and systems. It took me a long time to admit to myself that the level of control I wanted and desired simply couldn't exist. Governments had been promising to act on climate change for twenty years, and precisely nothing had happened. All of the trends, from extinction to soil erosion to ocean acidification to rainforest destruction, were going in the wrong direction, fast. We – the greens – knew what needed to be done, but had no power to make it happen. It wasn't working. I looked around me, at the diminishing natural beauty and its accelerating destruction, and I despaired.

*

A few things saved me, eventually, from this despair. One of them was a geological, or even universal, perspective. We tend to look at the world through an anthropocentric lens: human concerns are foremost in our vision, bounded by our short lives and our everyday needs and desires. Among those desires is a concern that what we have always known as 'nature' should continue as we have always known it. But nature has taken many forms. For the vast majority of its existence, 'nature' here on Earth consisted only of single-celled organisms. The brief period of climatic stability in which human civilisations have evolved is just that: a brief period. It is not any kind of norm, for there is no norm. Had it not been for the great oxygen catastrophe or the asteroid impact that wiped out the dinosaurs or who knows how many other such episodes, none of us would be here to agonise about the latest turbulent episode in the history of this planet. Why should the state of the planet to which we have adapted survive for ever? Nothing does. The Earth is a process as much as a thing: it is constantly changing. At this period in its history, we are the force tipping it into a new state. Now we are going to have to live with that state, whatever it brings – if we can.

All of which brings me, by a long and winding road, to Buddhism. Having skulked around on the edges of Buddhist thinking for many years, mostly unknowingly, it was only last year that I attended my first retreat. I didn't have any expectations: there was just a draw. But something was opened up to me during that five days of silence and contemplation and self-questioning. I realised, as I had never realised before, that the world and my perception of the world were not the same thing.

As I write it down now, it seems embarrassingly obvious, but there is a difference between knowing something intellectually and knowing it at this deeper level. I look at a forest. You look at a forest. We see different things. Perhaps one of us sees planking or sawdust or biological diversity or spiritual retreat or silence or rare insect life or certain mosses or a quality of light. Yet none of what we see has any relevance to the forest itself, or any of the organisms that make up its whole. It is just what it is. It is just there.

What does this mean? What it has meant for me is that I am now able to begin – only to begin, mind – separating reality from my view of it, and to understand the emotional projections that I overlay onto the world I walk through. One of those projections is a sense of what 'nature' is and should be, and how I should be able to help maintain it in a certain state. Nature itself, meanwhile, has no sense of that state. It has no sense that it is 'nature' at all. 'Nature' is made up of a vast and detailed complex of living beings doing what they do. Our self-consciousness, and our needs, are part of that complex. But nature doesn't need us, and 'extinction' as a concept is something that only humans worry about.

It is hard for us to take in the reality that Earth is an extinction machine, and it has been here before. It doesn't need us, and we cannot control it. The 'ecological crisis' we hear so much about, and that I have written so much about and worked to stave off – well, who says it is a 'crisis'? Humans do – and educated, socially concerned humans at that. For the Earth itself, the Holocene Extinction is not a 'crisis' – it is just another shift. Who determined that the planet should remain in the state which humans need and prefer? Is this not a form of clinging to mutable things, and one that is destined to make us unhappy? When we campaign to 'save the Earth' what are we really trying to save? And which Earth?

And yet. And yet, something I have come to understand slowly over my lifetime is that nature, Earth, the world – whatever you call it – is not simply something I am *on* but something I *am*. It is not outside of me, it is me, and I am it. There is no outside. 'Nature' as a concept has always been flawed. Many traditional societies had no word for 'nature' as something separate from humanity, because there was no obvious reason to separate humans from everything else that lived. There still isn't. Felt experiences of deep connection with all life are a central part of virtually all spiritual traditions, and with good reason: nature is us, and we are nature. The poet Robinson Jeffers described one of these epiphanic experiences powerfully in his verse drama *The Tower Beyond Tragedy*:

. . . I entered the life of the brown forest
And the great life of the ancient peaks, the patience of
*   stone, I felt the changes in the veins*
In the throat of the mountain, a grain in many centuries,
*   we have our own time, not yours; and I was the stream*
Draining the mountain woods; and I the stag drinking,
*   and I was the stars*
Boiling with light, wandering alone, each one the lord of
*   his own summit; and I was the darkness*
Outside the stars I included them, they were part of me . . .
. . . how can I express the excellence I have found, that has
*   no color but clearness;*
No honey but ecstasy . . .

I can understand and be awed by the ever-changing nature of this ever-changing Earth. I can appreciate my own smallness and know the importance of not clinging to temporary states. I can sometimes chide myself for my arrogance in assuming that what I appreciate as 'nature' is some unchanging state that should be preserved for my benefit, or even that of my species. Every extinction, after all, is also an opportunity. If the dinosaurs had survived, there would have been no humans. Everything changes, and the changes are not always pretty. Who said they had to be pretty?

But when all this is said, and because I am part of this Earth and not outside of it, if I see an old-growth forest being logged, I will want to lie down in front of the logging trucks. If I see a river being poisoned, I will want to stop it from happening. I can't abide factory farms or oil terminals or the destruction of clean air and open space. I have a sense of ecological justice that comes from something far deeper than mere principle. Because I am here, because I am nature, because I am Earth, these things, to me, are a violation of something sacred. And this sense of violation comes with a strong desire to try to prevent such wrongs from being enacted, even if the trying may in the end turn out to be futile.

How to square this circle, if it is a circle at all? It was one of the questions I asked the teacher at that retreat last year. The world may be ever-changing, I said, and my perception of it may not relate in any way to its reality. Yet when I look through the window at this wild landscape, I know that I would want to protect it if it were threatened. I feel a sense of what nature needs and what my duty is. What is the reality of this? Is it an illusion I should try not to cling to – and if it is, does a Buddhist response demand passivity in the face of destruction because clinging causes pain? Can this be right? How could it be right?

And the teacher, who was from the Chan/Zen tradition, said simply: sit with it. Sit with what is, and what you are, and watch it. If you are concerned about the forest, go to the forest, sit with the forest – and pay attention. And then you may know what to do.

I have always remembered this response. It reminded me of the deep sanity of the Buddhist worldview – the connected coolness beyond both emotion and reason that attracted me, I think, to begin with. Sit with the forest. Sitting with the forest is what I have been doing all my life. I have long felt that there is a language we civilised humans have forgotten how to speak. The spiritual writer and thinker Thomas Berry called this the 'great conversation', and he was clear about its significance:

> We are talking only to ourselves. We are not talking to the rivers, we are not listening to the wind and stars. We have broken the great conversation. By breaking that conversation we have shattered the universe. All the disasters that are happening now are a consequence of that spiritual 'autism'.

Any worldview that makes sense, I think now, must orbit around compassion. This is the other great lesson that Buddhism has taught me. Compassion comes, when it comes, from sitting with things, from slowing down, and paying attention to them and their needs. That applies, I would say, as much to non-human life as it does to our relationships with other people. Sitting with other beings, sitting with other people until you are beyond your mere self and can begin to contemplate theirs – this seems to me to be the still point of the turning world. It is not the end of the matter – it may be only the beginning. But it is a beginning.

*

There is one story about the life of the Buddha that has always fascinated me. Gautama is seated beneath the bodhi tree, having attained his enlightenment. Mara, the personification of demonic temptation, demands that Gautama produce a witness to confirm his Buddhahood. Gautama simply reaches down and touches the soil he sits on. The Earth is my witness, he says. Mara vanishes.

What does this mean? I'm no scholar, but I can say what it means to me: it means that if you make nature your witness, and if you act as a witness for nature too, there is a truth to be found. It even means, perhaps, that the ultimate truth – the ultimate witness to who we are – comes from the Earth itself. When you sit with the Earth, when you make it your witness and when you act as witness for it – what do you see? What are you compelled to do? These are questions that take us beyond political stances, beyond principles, beyond arguments about engagement or detachment. They are questions, it seems to me, that can never be answered in any way other than the strictly personal. Sitting or acting; engagement or retreat; perhaps there need be no contradiction.

A great change is under way, across the Earth. We cannot prevent it now, and its outcomes are not going to be pretty for much of humanity. The nature of nature has always been change, which means that death – and rebirth – will always be with us, and that rebirth may take forms we do not recognise and did not expect. You are part of this process, and so am I, and this time around we are the cause of it too. The future offers chaos, uncertainty, loss. To deny this is to deny reality. To pretend we have more control than we have, and to cling to glib 'solutions' as if the world were a maths puzzle we could solve with the right equations, is a similar form of denial. There is an abyss opening up before us. It challenges everything we thought we knew about our culture and about nature. We need to look into it and concentrate on what we can see.

'Sit with it,' the teacher said. It is a common Zen response, and though some may choose to see it as a kind of shoulder-shrugging, to me it looks like the opposite. What it really says is: *pay attention.* Our culture is hopeless at paying attention. It glorifies action and belittles contemplation. Responses to the ecocide currently unfurling around us are usually couched in aggressive demands for immediate 'action' – any action, it seems, however ineffective, is better than none. But it doesn't work like that.

My years in green activism showed me that false hope is worse than no hope, and that ineffective action leads only to despair, particularly if frantic movement is a substitute for facing up to the realities of our limited powers. Sooner or later, that dam will burst. Before you can act on anything with effectiveness, you have to understand it – and that is where the sitting comes in. That is where the attention matters. That is when the stripping back of your self before the indifference of nature will come to serve you.

What happens if you sit with the Earth? If you reach down and touch it, if you call it as your witness? What happens if you let your own needs and demands fall away, and see the world outside you for what it is? I would suggest that, with the right quality of attention, we may come to know what is right for us as individuals, and what we can usefully do. This doesn't mean that all will be well. All will not be well. It doesn't mean we will necessarily end up any less confused or conflicted, either. It doesn't mean we will never again experience the despair of knowing what we have done and what we are still doing and of all the things we are losing and can never bring back.

But it does mean, or it could, that we are able to hold those feelings within us, to understand them and maybe reconcile them. It does mean that we can be done with denial and projection and false hope and false hopelessness. If we sit with the Earth, with the trees and the soil and the wind and the mist, and pay attention, we may know what to do and how to begin doing it, whatever burden we carry with us as we walk.

Tricycle, 2015

Singing to the Forest

We had climbed, slowly, to a high mountain ridge. We were two young Englishmen who were not supposed to be here – journalism was forbidden – and four local guides, members of the Lani tribe. Our guides were moving us around the highlands of West Papua, taking us to meet people who could tell us about their suffering at the hands of the occupying Indonesian army.

The mountain ridge was covered in deep, old rainforest, as was the rest of the area we had walked through. This forest, to the Lani, was home. In the forest they hunted, gathered food, built their homes, lived. The forest was not a recreation or a resource: there was nothing romantic about it, nothing to debate. It was just life.

Now, as we reached the top of the ridge, a break in the trees opened up and we saw miles of unbroken green mountains rolling away before us to the horizon. It was a breathtaking sight. As I watched, our four guides lined up along the ridge and, facing the mountains, they sang. They sang a song to the forest whose words I didn't understand, but whose meaning was clear enough. It was a song of thanks; a song of belonging.

To the Lani, I learned later, the forest lived. This was no metaphor. The place itself, in which their people had lived for millennia, was not an inanimate 'environment', a mere backdrop for human activity. It was part of that activity. It was a great being, and to live as part of it was to be in a constant exchange with it. And so they sang to it; sometimes, it sang back.

When European minds experience this kind of thing, they are never quite sure to do with it. It's been so long since we in the West had a sense that we dwelled in a living landscape, that we don't have the words to frame what we see. Too often, we go in one of two directions, either sentimentalising the experience or dismissing it as superstition.

To us, the wild places around us (if there are any left) are 'resources' to be utilised. We argue constantly about how best to utilise them – should we log this forest, or turn it into a national park? – but only the bravest or the most foolish would suggest that it might not be our decision to make. To modern people, the world we walk through is not an animal, a being, a living presence; it is a machine, and our task is to learn how it works, the better to use it for our own, human, ends.

The notion that the non-human world is largely inanimate is often represented as 'scientific' or 'rational', but it is really more like a modern superstition. 'It is just like Man's vanity and impertinence,' wrote Mark Twain, 'to call an animal dumb because it is dumb to his dull perceptions.' We might say the same about a forest; and science, interestingly, might turn out to be on our side.

In recent years, several studies have demonstrated that plants, for example, communicate with each other in ways that seem to point towards some degree of self-awareness. They release pheromones to warn of insect attacks, and other plants respond. They signal to each other using a series of electrical impulses not dissimilar to that of an animal's nervous system. They send out airborne distress signals to insect predators that feed on the plant-eaters threatening them.

Underground, meanwhile, are the mycelia: huge fungal networks connecting the roots of thousands of plants and trees. The more mycelia are studied, the more intriguing they appear. Once thought to be a simple means of nutrient exchange, they are now beginning to look like complex systems of inter-plant communication. Mycologist Paul Stamets, who has spent his life studying them, calls mycelia a 'collective fungal consciousness'. Ecologist Stephan Harding believes they 'possess an eerie intelligence, and probably a peculiar sense of self to boot'.

The supposedly secular West still clings to the Abrahamic notion that only humans possess consciousness – or souls – and that this gives us the right or the duty to run the world. The scientists investigating animal and plant consciousness, though, may be taking us back to older ways of seeing by very modern means. Primitive savages who sing songs to the forest may not be primitive or savage after all. They may simply have retained an understanding that human-centred, urban people have forgotten: that the forest is, indeed, alive. And not only the forest. The living world around us may turn out to be much more sentient, aware, conscious and connected than we have allowed ourselves to believe.

As a writer, I wonder what our writing would look like if we took this notion seriously. I wonder, in particular, what our fiction – our stories – would look like. That the world is a machine is one story; that the world is alive and aware is another. The latter story has probably been taken for granted by the majority of human societies throughout history. The former has really taken root only in ours: post-Enlightenment, industrial Western culture, now becoming global culture. The results of it – climate change, mass extinction, factory farming, the usual litany of horrors – should be enough to make us wonder if this story is badly constructed, badly told – or just plain wrong.

How do writers tell stories in the West in the early twenty-first century? Mostly through novels. The internet, and the global capitalism it serves so well, may be putting the boot into traditional literary life, but nothing has yet supplanted the novel as the primary form through which long, written stories are brought to us. Rightly or wrongly, we still take novels seriously; we still read them. Some of us still write them, though we're not always sure why.

But what story do they tell? The novel is an artefact of Western individualism. Novels really came into their own in Europe with the rise of the commercial bourgeoisie; with empire and global trade, with cities and science and reason, with the notion of humans as primary actors in the world's drama. The same society that gave us the concept of the world as an inanimate backdrop to human activity gave us the novels that catalogued that story.

Most classic novels in the Western canon are examinations of the human psyche, or the relationships between small groups of people and their societies. They are studies of the individual human mind. But what about the mind of the world itself and how that manifests? If awareness, consciousness, feelings – life – all extend far beyond the human domain, why do novels continue to behave as if humans were the only actors? Why do we turn over the same exhausted soil again and again? What would a novel look like if it were written by someone who sang to the forest, and believed it sang back?

Robert Graves, in his poetic manifesto *The White Goddess*, wrote that modern poetry's function was to lay bare the results of humanity's break from the rest of nature:

> Once a warning to man that he must keep in harmony with the family of living creatures among which he was born . . . it is now a reminder that he has disregarded the warning, turned the house upside down by capricious experiments in science, philosophy and industry, and brought ruin upon himself and his family.

If this is true of poetry, it is true of fiction too. Perhaps, in a century's time, any literary critics still clinging to their positions as the seas rise around them will see the work we writers produce today as a useful historical record of our society's insanity. Because we have cut ourselves off from everything else that lives, and because we don't believe that it does live, we have ended up talking only to ourselves. We have ended what Thomas Berry called 'the great conversation' between humans and other forms of life. We are becoming human narcissists, entombed in our cities, staring into our screens, seeing our faces and our minds reflected back and believing this is all there is. And outside the forests fall, the ice melts, the corals die back and the extinctions roll on; but we keep writing our love letters to ourselves, oblivious.

What might the alternative look like? Perhaps the poets can see this better than the novelists. Robinson Jeffers, poet of the California cliffs, spent his life trying to transcribe the song of the living world and make it fit for human ears. He ends his poem 'Carmel Point' with a prescription:

> *We must uncenter our minds from ourselves;*
> *We must unhumanize our views a little, and become*
>   *confident*
> *As the rock and ocean that we were made from.*

The ecological crisis we have spawned will 'unhumanize' our views for us, whether we like it or not. The notions that only humans matter, or that humans are in control, even of themselves, are unlikely to outlast this century. It seems a good time for writers to 'become confident as the rock and ocean', and to begin writing about the rock and ocean as if they had a part to play. The novel looks pretty exhausted these days. Could this be its new frontier?

There have always been novels in which the landscape, and the non-human creatures in it, have played a powerful part. Just looking along my limited bookshelf I can see Thomas Hardy's *Jude the Obscure* and *The Return of the Native*, in which the rural landscapes of his still pre-modern Wessex are as memorable as his human characters; Emily Brontë's *Wuthering Heights*, whose wild Pennine uplands experience moods as dark as that of Heathcliff; Ursula Le Guin's *Earthsea* trilogy, set in a fictional archipelago whose islands are as distinctive as any on our planet; and D. H. Lawrence's *The Plumed Serpent*, set in a dark pagan Mexico whose taste lingers in the mind longer than its storyline. More recently, and more locally, fiction by young writers such as Ben Myers and Daisy Johnson weave stories around wild English landscapes that act as ominous backdrops to the human stories they tell; stories that seem smaller as a result, and thus more urgent.

A powerful landscape is one thing, though; a sentient landscape is another. A question that has been jabbing at me for some time is: how could a novel be written in which a living landscape was not just a backdrop, but a *character*: an actor in the drama, rather than its scenery? Are there novels in which non-human places are sensate? In which the mind of the world is made manifest in the places its human characters walk through? Having just tried to write one myself, I have been looking for precedents. So far, I have discovered only two writers who seem to even approach the question.

The first is William Golding, in his 1956 novel *Pincher Martin*. The eponymous sailor, blown into the sea when his boat is torpedoed during World War Two, washes up on the only land for miles around: a great, jagged, black rock, which juts above the waves. For the next two hundred pages there is only Martin, the gulls, the anemones, and the rock, which seems, at first, to be simply an inanimate object. But the rock is something more.

It's hard to explain why without ruining the novel's startling conclusion, but it's safe to say that the rock is also a conduit for a voice, a confessional, a testing ground, a judge. The rock is waiting and watching, and the man on the rock is refusing to be part of it, refusing to believe that there is anything outside his own self. Whether he likes it or not, the rock has a lesson for him, which he is going to have to learn.

Perhaps the writer who has done most to explore the notion of a sensate landscape, though, is Alan Garner. The living, jolting, magical power of places is at the heart of almost everything he has written for the last five decades. A moor, a hill, a ridge, a wood: in Garner's books these are not 'landscapes' but conduits to an older, wilder magic. History tugs at them, and they tug in turn at the feet of the innocent people who happen to walk across them.

In Garner's 2003 novel *Thursbitch*, the Pennine valley that gives the book its title links two people separated by time, one in the eighteenth century, one living today. Garner's deep knowledge and understanding of the place and its history is typical of his work, but so too is the sense that this landscape is hungry: it wants something; it is almost toying with people. It is as if the place has brought the book's human actors together for a reason: as if some riddle must be solved, some destiny fulfilled. Ancient, pagan energies seem to emanate from the old valley, drawing people in across time, weaving the threads, constructing a pattern that humans may always be too small to comprehend.

Are there other novels, and other novelists, which make the world beyond the human, the land itself, a living part of their story? Maybe there are dozens, which I haven't come across in my limited reading. If not, maybe the lack reflects a peculiarity of the English-language novel, or of the European novel, or of the rational, liberal, urban middle-class minds that tend to write them. Or maybe it is just impossible for any of us, ultimately, to 'unhumanize our views', any more than a rabbit could unrabbitise or a worm unworm theirs. Maybe we can only ever speak to, and of, ourselves.

But I'm not so sure. Writing a story is an act of projection. We imagine what it would be like to be this character, to live in this time, to be in this situation, and if we can't do that well, our books won't work. If we can do that well, why can't we make the same imaginative leap and take ourselves out of our humanity? Is it harder to imagine a sensate land-scape, or the worldview of another living being, than it is to imagine life on a Martian colony or in a fifteenth-century village?

Probably. Still, that's not a reason not to try. Glorious failures are always more interesting than unambitious suc-cesses. And surely the times demand it. 'The universe is not a machine after all,' proclaimed D. H. Lawrence, a man who never stopped paying attention to it; 'it's alive and kicking.' Kicking and singing and watching, too. Who will write its story?

Guardian, 2016

Planting Trees in the Anthropocene

A Conspiracy Theory

I wish I wish I wish in vain
I wish I were a maid again.
But a maid again I never shall be
'Till apples grow on an orange tree.
Traditional Northumbrian song

There was something undefined and yet
    complete-in-itself,
Born before Heaven-and-Earth.
Silent and boundless,
Standing alone without change,
Yet pervading all without fail,
It may be regarded as the Mother of the world.
Tao Teh Ching 25

Slit-planting is the easiest way to plant a bare root tree. It needs to be done in winter, sometime between November and March, when both the tree and the soil are dormant. We planted ours in February, just within the window. It was hard work: harder than I realised at the time. I am writing this in June, and my body still hasn't recovered. My left arm is partly crippled at the moment by tendonitis, and my lower back is bad on some days and not so bad on others. My fingers and wrists begin to ache and tingle if I demand too much from them. This means that the acres of grass I have to scythe on my land are going uncut, and the place is running wild. I think I'm going to need to ask our neighbour to graze his horses in our field again, because I can't do much else with it this year. My hands and my arms are currently not suited to serious physical work, as a direct result of my winter toils with the trees. That, and over twenty years of typing words like this into computers, which has frazzled the tendons and the nerves in my forearms possibly beyond repair. The spade and the keyboard are two very different tools, but one thing they have in common is their ability to break the human body.

We planted around five hundred small trees. Most of them will end up in our woodstove: the idea is to be self-sufficient in household heating as soon as possible. For this purpose, we've planted several uneven blocks of birch, poplar and willow, which will have a coppice cycle of six or seven years if we're lucky. On top of that, we've put in about a hundred sticks of basket willow, in differing colours. These are for utility too, I suppose, but of the pleasurable kind: basket-weaving is my wife's new passion. We've also planted three hedges of native trees – rowan, more birch, spindle, holly, wild cherry, hazel, oak – to create windbreaks, shield us from the lane in front of the house and make some kind of offering for the birds around here. Perhaps it will distract their attention from our vegetable garden, which they are currently digging up daily. I like birds, but my patience is not infinite.

Finally, we put in a small plantation of birch. I love birch groves. Ours is only a few metres square, but I've made a fire pit in the middle of it, and maybe in ten years I'll be able to sit around it and pretend I'm on the Russian steppe. I don't know why I would want to pretend that, but I do. That wild, white emptiness stretching for miles to a low purple horizon: I've never been there, but I can see it from here.

The real work was in clearing the ground, most of which was covered thickly with a deep tangle of brambles and suckering blackthorns. When we moved to this little patch of land, we came with ideals, and one of them was to do our work by hand, with as little impact as possible. So we laid into the thorns and brambles, which must have been growing for decades, with scythes and mattocks and spades and machetes. It took weeks and weeks. The scratches were deep. The industrial-strength gloves we bought were torn to shreds. More than one mattock handle was broken. I have never seen suckers so thick or long, or root balls so deep and woody. Even after weeks of clearing the ground by hand, we still had to hire a digger for a day to tear out the deepest of the roots and make the ground fit for planting.

After that, the planting itself was a doddle. To slit-plant a tree, you just push your spade into the ground up to the end of the blade, wiggle it back and forth until you have a wide enough slit and then simply drop the tree root into it. It takes a bit of practice to get the right angle, but once you know how, you can make your slit, drop in the tree, tamp it down with the heel of your boot, and hey presto: a baby tree, reaching up to the winter sky. You cover the ground around the tree with newspaper, and then pile wet straw on top of that to mulch it. Finally, if your land attracts both rabbits and hares, which ours does, you wind a plastic spiral tree guard around the tiny trunk, and fortify it with a garden cane against the Atlantic winds.

Do that five hundred times, and you have a little forest. Better, you have a forest planted in a low-impact and ecological way. You have an endless supply of sustainable fuel for your sustainable household, and you have used minimal dirty fossil fuels in order to create it. You have taken some wasteland and made it into a diverse ecosystem. You have created a closed-loop system, and a mini carbon sink. You have also crippled yourself. But it was worth it.

At least, that's what I thought I would be telling myself at this stage. But I'm not so sure any more.

I don't mean that it wasn't worth it. I would have liked to have done it without the consequent pain, but I don't regret putting the trees in. I love watching them grow, I love the fact that we've grown them, and I think they will enhance the place. This is the kind of thing we came here to do, and compared with a lot of what is done to agricultural land in this country and so many others, it is a good thing. Maybe I can grow alongside these trees, and learn a little patience from them. Maybe we can leave this place better than we found it. That's the idea.

But I'm kidding myself if I think this was a 'low-impact' enterprise, and I'm not just talking about the impact on my musculoskeletal system. It was a two-hour journey in my diesel-powered camper van to collect the trees in the first place. A heavy-duty mini-digger used up a day's worth of fossil fuel to heave the old root balls out of our land. And those are just the most obvious examples of our reliance on not-very-sustainable industrial technologies to put our little forest in. Consider the simple tools: the spade, the mattock, the machete, the scythe. All of them made of steel whose ore was dragged up from some mountain somewhere and smelted, shaped and tempered in a factory, then fixed to a machine-tooled handle made of wood from who-knows-where and shipped to wherever I bought them from. All of them, like my gardening gloves and my wellies and my raincoat, and the plastic tree spirals and the newspaper and even the straw, products of a globe-spanning techno-industrial economy, which helped us to plant our low-impact trees in our low-impact garden.

Then, of course, there is the awkward fact that in order to plant these trees we had to cut down a lot of . . . trees. The trees, or bushes, that we chopped down were suckering blackthorn and bramble, mainly. They were not useful or attractive to us, whereas the ones we planted were. I give this an ecological gloss by talking up the fact that we have planted native species, and a good diversity of them at that, but whichever way I cut it, we have cleared a wilderness in order to plant crops. The product of those crops might be firewood or basket willow or natural beauty or human contentment or protection against the elements, but they are crops nevertheless, and the things they replaced were wild plants growing without any human intervention.

It turns out that living a simpler life can be quite complicated.

*

I was about a quarter of the way into *What Technology Wants* before I realised I was reading a religious text. It was quite a revelation. *What Technology Wants* is a book published a few years back by Kevin Kelly, co-founder of *Wired* magazine and a significant spokesman for what we might call the Silicon Valley Mindset. It takes us on a journey through the historical development of technology and into a future in which, Kelly believes, technology will be a living force that controls our destiny.

The book starts by leading us on a journey through the development of technology, or perhaps, more accurately, the *idea* of technology. The idea, it turns out, is a fairly new one. Though humans have been using tools since they first dug holes with sticks, and though the Greeks and the Romans invented everything from iron welding and the bellows through to blown glass and watermills more than two millennia ago, there was no sense that this collection of useful artefacts was anything more than the sum of its parts. 'Technology could be found everywhere in the ancient world except in the minds of humans,' writes Kelly. That changed in 1802, when, at the height of the Industrial Revolution, German economics professor Johann Beckmann coined the word 'technology' to refer to the 'systemic order' of tools and machines that were beginning to take over many of the functions previously assumed by humans.

That was just over two hundred years ago. Before that, a spade and a mattock were just a spade and a mattock: useful additions to life, which made work easier. After that, they were part of something bigger, at least in Kelly's telling. Kelly is a techno-utopian and, to him, this thing called 'technology' is not just a collection of tools and machines but, as he puts it, 'a living force'. He calls this force 'the technium', and he describes it like this:

The technium extends beyond shiny hardware to include culture, art, social institutions, and intellectual creations of all types. It includes tangibles like software, law, and philosophical concepts. And most important, it includes the generated impulses of our inventions to encourage more toolmaking, more technology invention, and more self-enhancing connections.

This technium, explains Kelly, is a 'global, massively inter-connected system of technology vibrating around us', which is taking on its own life and its own mind. It is this last claim that makes his book so interesting. You can find plenty of people who will argue, like Kelly, that technology will save us from pretty much every problem on Earth, if we would only trust it. Techno-utopianism is a subset of the contem-porary religion of Progress, into which we are all baptised at birth. If Progress is God, technology is the messiah come to do His will on Earth. In this reading, the benefits of mod-ern technology – fewer deaths in childbirth, dental hygiene, the ability to Tweet a picture of what you had for breakfast to someone on the other side of the planet – are talked up, while its drawbacks – nuclear bombs, mass extinction, cli-mate change, viral videos of Korean pop hits – are glossed over. This is the standard narrative of modernity, and argu-ing against it is likely to see you labelled a 'romantic Lud-dite' at best, and a reactionary hater of 'the poor' at worst.

This line, though, usually comes with a denial that our increasingly complex technologies could ever be anything other than inanimate servants. You will hear from its pro-ponents that 'technology is neutral', that 'technologies are neither good nor bad; it depends what we do with them', that 'no technology is inevitable; we're free to use the good ones and reject the bad ones'. This is where Kelly stands out, because he is having none of this. He shares with technology's sternest critics a controversial but, I think, correct perspective: that the huge and complex web of advanced technologies we have built around us is now so central to our lives, so complex and interconnected and fast-evolving, that it is becoming an autonomous thing, separate from humanity, though currently still dependent on it. This thing is the technium. And it has only just got started:

> After ten thousand years of slow evolution and two hundred years of incredible intricate exfoliation, the technium is maturing into its own thing. Its sustaining network of self-reinforcing processes and parts have given it a noticeable measure of autonomy. It may have once been as simple as an old computer program, merely parroting what we told it, but now it is more like a very complex organism that often follows its own urges.

Much of the rest of Kelly's book is dedicated to trying to prove his case that the technium is 'as great a force in our world as nature', and is similarly irresistible. As the book goes on, that case gets more and more daring. Kelly claims that the technium, like biological life, is a force of evolution. It predates the evolution of humanity, he says (pre-human and non-human animals were and are using tools too) and like biological evolution itself, its course is inevitable and teleological. Technological life, like biological life, tends towards more complexity, more interdependence and more intelligence, because 'technology and life share some fundamental essence'. We are now so symbiotic with technology, so dependent on it, that 'if all technology – very last knife and spear – were to be removed from this planet, our species would not last more than a few months'. This means that trying to resist the march of the technium is futile and self-defeating. Instead we must 'surrender to its advances' and 'listen to what it wants'. This will involve us giving up some measures of freedom but, in return, we shall 'unleash human potential', which will lead to 'deep progress' as we merge with machines and become greater than we could possibly imagine.

If this sounds like the marginal outpourings of a starry-eyed techno-creationist, it's worth understanding how influential Kelly and his co-thinkers are. His generation of Silicon Valley techno-hippies includes the late Steve Jobs, founder of Apple, the neo-green coterie who cluster around Stewart Brand, founder of the *Whole Earth Catalog*, and the influential booster of the post-human future Ray Kurzweil, whose techno-utopianism makes Kevin Kelly looked like a barefoot pilgrim.

Kurzweil is the most famous promoter of the concept of the 'Singularity', through which humanity will merge with machines to create a new super-species. Kurzweil thinks this will happen within his lifetime. He is looking forward to living for ever, and he is working on technologies that will enable much that is currently inanimate to become a living, web-embedded presence in the physical world.

In May 2015, he offered up a list of predictions as to where 'progress', enabled by the reach of the technium, would take us in the near future. Within a decade, he said, self-driving cars, communicating with each other and coordinating their own movements, would be ubiquitous on the roads. Before that, within five years, current internet search engines would begin to give way to algorithmic 'personal assistants', which could 'annotate reality' for you. They could 'listen in to a conversation, giving helpful hints', or even 'suggest an anecdote that would fit into your conversation in real-time'. Kurzweil is developing these programs himself at the moment, and he is optimistic that they will soon be with us.

Not long after, they will be followed by full-immersion virtual-reality computer games. 'To fully master the tactile sense, we have to actually tap into the nervous system,' he explains.

> We'll be able to send little devices, nanobots, into the brain and capillaries and they'll provide additional sensory signals, as if they were coming from your real senses. You could, for example, get together with a friend, even though you are hundreds of thousands of miles apart, and take a virtual walk on a virtual Mediterranean beach and hold their hand and feel the warm spray of the moist air in your face.

By 2040, even that will be bettered by the technium's ability to help us 'stay young for ever'. Once we can get 'little robots in the bloodstream that augment your immune system', immortality itself won't be far away.

Once upon a time, this kind of thing was held up by science-fiction writers as a warning about the dangers of human hubris. Today, Ray Kurzweil is Director of Engineering at Google. None of us should be in any doubt at this point: this is the future. It has been long planned, and it is under development. The technium is coming for you. How will you advance to meet it?

Being human is a challenge, but one of its upsides is the fascinating diversity of perspectives that human beings have. A dozen of us can look at one event, or consider one idea, and we can be planets apart in how we see it and in what conclusions we draw. When Ray Kurzweil considers inserting tiny robots into his brain so that he can be dropped, *Matrix*-like, into a perfect simulation of a beach walk with a distant friend, he presumably finds it thrilling. I find it horrifying; but I can understand it. When I was a teenager, I had my head in a science-fiction book most of the time. I don't think there are many sci-fi classics I didn't read, and I was looking forward, as Ray presumably is, to living for ever and having robot servants and slingshotting around the moons of Jupiter while I watched attack ships on fire off the shoulder of Orion. Seen from one perspective – excited, can-do, replete with a certain kind of uncomplicated modernist optimism – there is nothing more thrilling than this stuff. Ray Kurzweil and Kevin Kelly still see it from this perspective. Why don't I?

I ask myself this question sometimes, and I think, in the end, it's because I don't want to be liberated in the way that they do. *Liberation* is a word that occurs again and again in the writings of the apostles of the technium. In this reading, life is a project of progressive liberation, of the throwing off of shackles, of being the best we can be. Evolution is like a giant self-help manual. Ray Kurzweil wants to liberate us from 'the outdated software of our bodies'. Kevin Kelly wants to go even further: the technium, he says, can free us not only from our limiting physical frames, but from nature and time itself:

Technology's dominance ultimately stems not from its birth in human minds but from its origin in the same self-organisation that brought galaxies, planets, life, and minds into existence. It is part of a great asymmetrical arc that begins at the big bang and extends into ever more abstract and immaterial forms over time. The arc is the slow yet irreversible liberation from the ancient imperative of matter and energy.

Advanced technology, in other words, will one day liberate us from the universe. It's an astonishing claim, and it's worth dwelling on, because this is the point at which the technium becomes a religious concern. Kelly acknowledges that its advance will lead to – indeed, already is leading to – the 'erosion of the traditional self' and that the advance of the machine and our increasing dependence on it 'chips away at human dignity'. The ultimate endpoint of this is likely to be the abolition of humanity as we know it, but the flip side of the bargain is that this 'liberation' will lead to 'increasing the options, choices and possibilities' of all living things.

A transcendent force exists that is beyond the power and understanding of humanity, though it is also entwined closely with it. This force can liberate us from earthly misery and transport us into an eternal paradise in which we shall be changed, but only if we surrender to its will. Doesn't this sound like a certain kind of religious story? I can't help seeing the narrative being spun out by Kelly and Kurzweil and all of their Silicon Valley stablemates as a new story of silicon transcendence: a story, in the end, about the death of God and His replacement in the modern mind by machines that can do His, and humanity's, job better.

The technium will become God. Or perhaps God was always in the technium. Kelly seems to think so. In the last three pages of his book, something extraordinary happens: it's as if he can no longer contain himself, and what has been posing up to this point as an investigative enquiry into our relationship with technology becomes, rather like the technium itself, what it had always wanted to be: a mystical text. 'If there is a God,' writes Kelly, 'the arc of the technium is aimed right at him . . . the technium is the way the universe has engineered its own self-awareness . . . the smallest thought could not exist unless the entire universe and the laws of physics were in some way encouraging it.'

*

Planting my trees was a technological endeavour. In using even the basic tools, even the spade and the scythe and the mattock, I was locking myself into a global web of technological interdependence. Does that mean that the innocent project of planting trees is itself a part of the technium, rather than an escape from it? Kevin Kelly would say so, and in one sense he'd be right. There is no escape from our tools, from our technologies, from the part of ourselves that we have put into them. We are what we do and what we make and what we use, and everything is dependent on everything else.

But there is something missing from this perspective; some nuance, some flicker of truth. Yes, I was tied into the industrial economy when I planted my trees. But if the industrial economy were to disappear tomorrow, could I still plant them? Yes, I could, though I may not want to. Both may give you sore arms, but there is a difference between a keyboard and a spade. A spade can still be made fairly simply. It doesn't need constant energy to keep going. It can last a long time, if you treat it well, rather like your body. A keyboard and a spade are both products of an industrial economy, but not to the same extent, and they do not have the same purpose. One can exist independently, the other cannot. This might be a matter of degrees, but the degrees matter – and so does the intent.

There's another point too, though, and perhaps it is a more important one: nobody ever got addicted to a spade. Yet we are surely addicted to the technium. Walk down a street in any city and count the number of people whose eyes are glued to their smartphones as they walk. Sit in a cafe and count the number of two- and three-year-old kids who are staring at tablet computers instead of into the eyes of their equally net-bound parents. We are stuck in a web, caught in a net, and I'm not sure we could escape now if we wanted to. But we don't want to. Our astonishing ability to accept virtually anything the digital world throws at us without questioning its downside for an instant sometimes sends shivers down my spine. I may not share Kevin Kelly's perspective, but I think he is right about the nature of the technium. I think there is something bigger than us, rearranging itself around us now like a prison. It's a prison we don't seem to want to escape from, because there's so much fun to be had in it; and anyway if we did want to escape we couldn't, so why bother trying?

I don't want to sound as if I've read too much science fiction, but I'm on board with both Kelly and Kurzweil to this extent: this thing is bigger than us now. It is developing a degree of autonomy, and it is using us, somehow, to create itself. I know this sounds like a conspiracy theory, but it's not really a theory, it's more of a hunch: a conspiracy feeling. We are surrendering the freedom to be human in exchange for the freedom to live in confected dreams: dreams in which nature is dead, except for the pretty bits, and bad things never happen, and nobody dies, and there is nothing to life but entertainment and everything we see we can control, because we have created it. On Ray Kurzweil's Mediterranean beach, there will be no poisonous jellyfish, there will be no litter on the tide, and nobody will mug you as you walk home at dusk. Maybe we long for this pseudo-life. Perhaps we want the beauty and the transcendence without the darkness and the danger. Maybe that's what the promises of heaven were always about, in the end.

Nature itself, real nature, the one that evolved without us controlling it, is messy. For most of the history of civilisation we have had to fight it off. Planting trees is painful and clearing ground is backbreaking, yet it can offer us meaning. But maybe the technium, as it advances, will give us meaning, too: perhaps the nanobots in our brains will create a simulacrum of it in a virtual-reality nature in which we get all of the beauty and none of the cowshit on our boots. That, I suppose, is the dream. Transcendence without the effort. The business of being human without the work that brings it about. What is the project of modernity if it is not a product of liberating the individual from the mass, liberating the body from work and pain, liberating the mind from fear and confusion? Liberation, freedom, eternal life in a simulated heaven. God may be dead, but it seems religion isn't.

Still, there is more to the technium than its salvational draw. At its simplest, it promises us heaven here on Earth, and what it promises us goes with the grain of contemporary Western culture, which increasingly means global culture. In an age in which people conflate desires with rights, and in which whole generations have grown up seeing themselves as consumers in a marketplace, demanding their money's worth, it is well placed to deliver. Want to have babies at the age of seventy, or clone yourself, or create children from the genetic material of five different people, or have a nanobot resequence your genes so you can live to five hundred, or download your consciousness into a machine that will go on for ever? The technium is your friend. And who has the right to tell you that you can't do these things? Priests? Ethicists? Environmentalists? Luddites and reactionaries, all of them. If it is what you want, you should have it, because that is what freedom now means. How long can it be before cheating death becomes a human right?

Politically, the technium also looks well placed to satisfy the current cultural desire for total human equality. Advanced technology, combined with capitalist markets, is a far greater leveller of difference and distinction than communism ever was. It destroys cultural and geographical differences, abolishes traditions and creates a one-world factory floor cum marketplace in which everyone is equal in the eyes of the machine. Left to its own devices, the technium will doubtless abolish poverty, create gender and racial equality and remove any of the 'discriminations' associated with awkward, local, specific or traditional ways of being human in the world. Marx, I think, would have been impressed. If you have ever wondered why supposedly 'radical' thinkers on the left rarely question technology, your answer is here. If you seek a world of perfect sameness, the technium is poised to give it to you. The price it will extract will be the abolition of human nature. At the moment, it seems we are willing to pay it.

*

Sometimes I'm kept awake at night by a chicken-and-egg question: which came first, the science or the science fiction? It seems to me that my society is reaching towards a real-world version of the science-fictional universes that we grew up with. The robot butlers, the holodecks, the lunar colonies, the invisibility devices, the machines that do our thinking and even our moving for us: these are all on the drawing board, or at a later stage than that. Perhaps the science fiction was never fiction at all: perhaps it was a foreshadowing; the implanting in our minds of ideas that we would later bring to reality in the service of the Machine we are creating.

Kevin Kelly and Ray Kurzweil don't agree on everything, but what they do agree on seems to be shared by the team running Google, by the masters of the hyper-real universe who work in Silicon Valley, and by the intellectual classes across the Western world and increasingly beyond. What they agree on is that the future is hyper-digital, web-embedded and increasingly virtual. We are in for a world of wearable technology and smart homes, self-driving cars, synthetic lifeforms in the fields and forests and an accelerating merger between carbon and silicon, human and machine, natural and artificial, until the boundaries have blurred so much that nobody can tell the difference, and everyone has long since stopped caring. The geeks who run the world's biggest web corporations have this in common with the ranks of the neo-luddites: they all think the technium is coming, and none of them knows how to stop it. What they argue about is whether we should want to.

I'm sure it's unfair to Kevin Kelly, but halfway through his book I found myself suddenly remembering the anti-modern denunciations of Oliver Mellors, the randy gamekeeper in D. H. Lawrence's novel *Lady Chatterley's Lover*. I went to look up the exact words, and they made me smile:

> Motor-cars and cinemas and aeroplanes suck that last bit out of them. I tell you, every generation breeds a more rabbity generation, with India rubber tubing for guts and tin legs and tin faces. Tin people! It's all a steady sort of bolshevism just killing off the human thing, and worshipping the mechanical thing . . . All the modern lot get their real kick out of killing the old human feeling out of Man . . .

When I read Kelly on the technium or Kurzweil on the Singularity, when I hear Sergey Brin enthusing over his Google Glasses or see Mark Zuckerberg predicting wearable technology or smart fridges, I can't helping thinking how many more rabbity generations we are further on from old Mellors and his Lady. My generation 'needs' technologies my parents never did, and my children's will 'need' even more. Perhaps in the overdeveloped West we've just forgotten what it means to be human in the world. Or perhaps this is what it means to be human: innovating, remaking, building until the foundations give way. Perhaps we will all end up as tin people, or silicon people, all the old human feeling killed, and we'll not know that it was ever different. Perhaps that has already happened. Perhaps 'the mechanical thing' that Mellors could see being worshipped was the technium rising, building its walls, bricking us in.

Maybe Kevin Kelly would say that I have less faith in humanity than he does, but I think I have more. Being human is hard work. It hurts. Being a machine must be a lot easier. Maybe this explains the apparent desire of some of us to merge with our creations. We are becoming machines, and our machines are becoming gods; or we think they are. Or we want to think so. Kelly certainly does, and I suspect he is not alone. 'We can see more of God in a cell phone than in a tree frog,' he contends in his book's fascinating and disturbing climax:

> The phone extends the frog's four billion years of
> learning and adds the open-ended investigations of six
> billion human minds. Someday we may believe the most
> convivial technology we can make is not a testament
> to human ingenuity but a testament of the holy . . .
> the intricate, unfathomable layers of logic built up
> over a century, borrowed from rainforest ecosystems,
> and woven together into beauty by millions of active
> synthetic minds will say what redwoods say, only louder,
> more convincingly: 'Long before you were here, I am.'

It's a few weeks now since I began writing this essay. It's sunny this morning, beautifully so. There are three white mares cropping the grass in our field, and today I spent an hour mowing the grass around the young trees with my scythe. My elbow still hurts, but I have found some exercises that seem to be improving it. We dug a pond next to the alder trees last week and it's full of water beetles already. I don't know where they came from. Nature's ability to rejuvenate itself, to be born and born and born again never ceases to come in at me when I least expect it.

You can spend too much time with thoughts of the future. The future, after all, doesn't exist. Step away from those thoughts, get blisters on the heels of your hands and yes, mess up your arms, and you begin to see what actually does. Your perspective adjusts. Today, sitting here in the sun, I can't see anything of God in my mobile phone, but He, She or It seems to be dancing all over the buttercups and red clover in the meadow before me. Watching the dance, I think we have far less control over the world than Ray Kurzweil believes we do, and that the future is less ordained than Kevin Kelly wants it to be. I don't know what's coming, but I just saw a heron fly past my open window on its way to the river. The grasses are moving in the wind that is coming in from the west. Soon enough, we'll see.

Dark Mountain, issue 8, 2015

EPILOGUE

Uncivilisation

The Dark Mountain manifesto
Paul Kingsnorth and Dougald Hine

REARMAMENT

These grand and fatal movements toward death: the
   grandeur of the mass
Makes pity a fool, the tearing pity
For the atoms of the mass, the persons, the victims, makes
   it seem monstrous
To admire the tragic beauty they build.
It is beautiful as a river flowing or a slowly gathering
Glacier on a high mountain rock-face,
Bound to plow down a forest, or as frost in November,
The gold and flaming death-dance for leaves,
Or a girl in the night of her spent maidenhood, bleeding
   and kissing.
I would burn my right hand in a slow fire
To change the future ... I should do foolishly. The beauty
   of modern
Man is not in the persons but in the
Disastrous rhythm, the heavy and mobile masses, the
   dance of the
Dream-led masses down the dark mountain.
   Robinson Jeffers, 1935

I: WALKING ON LAVA

> The end of the human race will be that it will eventually die of civilisation.
>
> *Ralph Waldo Emerson*

Those who witness extreme social collapse at first hand seldom describe any deep revelation about the truths of human existence. What they do mention, if asked, is their surprise at how easy it is to die.

The pattern of ordinary life, in which so much stays the same from one day to the next, disguises the fragility of its fabric. How many of our activities are made possible by the impression of stability that pattern gives? So long as it repeats, or varies steadily enough, we are able to plan for tomorrow as if all the things we rely on and don't think about too carefully will still be there. When the pattern is broken, by civil war or natural disaster or the smaller-scale tragedies that tear at its fabric, many of those activities become impossible or meaningless, while simply meeting needs we once took for granted may occupy much of our lives.

What war correspondents and relief workers report is not only the fragility of the fabric, but the speed with which it can unravel. As we write this, no one can say with certainty where the unravelling of the financial and commercial fabric of our economies will end. Meanwhile, beyond the cities, unchecked industrial exploitation frays the material basis of life in many parts of the world, and pulls at the ecological systems which sustain it.

Precarious as this moment may be, however, an awareness of the fragility of what we call civilisation is nothing new.

'Few men realise', wrote Joseph Conrad in 1896, 'that their life, the very essence of their character, their capabilities and their audacities, are only the expression of their belief in the safety of their surroundings.' Conrad's writings exposed the civilisation exported by European imperialists to be little more than a comforting illusion, not only in the dark, unconquerable heart of Africa, but in the whited sepulchres of their capital cities. The inhabitants of that civilisation believed 'blindly in the irresistible force of its institutions and its morals, in the power of its police and of its opinion', but their confidence could be maintained only by the seeming solidity of the crowd of like-minded believers surrounding them. Outside the walls, the wild remained as close to the surface as blood under skin, though the city-dweller was no longer equipped to face it directly.

Bertrand Russell caught this vein in Conrad's worldview, suggesting that the novelist 'thought of civilised and morally tolerable human life as a dangerous walk on a thin crust of barely cooled lava which at any moment might break and let the unwary sink into fiery depths'. What both Russell and Conrad were getting at was a simple fact which any historian could confirm: human civilisation is an intensely fragile construction. It is built on little more than belief: belief in the rightness of its values; belief in the strength of its system of law and order; belief in its currency; above all, perhaps, belief in its future.

Once that belief begins to crumble, the collapse of a civilisation may become unstoppable. That civilisations fall, sooner or later, is as much a law of history as gravity is a law of physics. What remains after the fall is a wild mixture of cultural debris, confused and angry people whose certainties have betrayed them, and those forces which were always there, deeper than the foundations of the city walls: the desire to survive and the desire for meaning.

It is, it seems, our civilisation's turn to experience the in-rush of the savage and the unseen; our turn to be brought up short by contact with untamed reality. There is a fall coming. We live in an age in which familiar restraints are being kicked away, and foundations snatched from under us. After a quarter-century of complacency, in which we were invited to believe in bubbles that would never burst, prices that would never fall, the end of history, the crude repack-aging of the triumphalism of Conrad's Victorian twilight – Hubris has been introduced to Nemesis. Now a familiar human story is being played out. It is the story of an em-pire corroding from within. It is the story of a people who believed, for a long time, that their actions did not have con-sequences. It is the story of how that people will cope with the crumbling of their own myth. It is our story.

This time, the crumbling empire is the unassailable global economy, and the brave new world of consumer democracy being forged worldwide in its name. Upon the indestruct-ibility of this edifice we have pinned the hopes of this latest phase of our civilisation. Now, its failure and fallibility ex-posed, the world's elites are scrabbling frantically to buoy up an economic machine which, for decades, they told us needed little restraint, for restraint would be its undoing. Uncountable sums of money are being funnelled upwards in order to prevent an uncontrolled explosion. The machine is stuttering and the engineers are in panic. They are won-dering if perhaps they do not understand it as well as they imagined. They are wondering whether they are controlling it at all or whether, perhaps, it is controlling them.

Increasingly, people are restless. The engineers group themselves into competing teams, but neither side seems to know what to do, and neither seems much different from the other. Around the world, discontent can be heard. The extremists are grinding their knives and moving in as the machine's coughing and stuttering exposes the inadequacies of the political oligarchies who claimed to have everything in hand. Old gods are rearing their heads, and old answers: revolution, war, ethnic strife. Politics as we have known it totters, like the machine it was built to sustain. In its place could easily arise something more elemental, with a dark heart.

As the financial wizards lose their powers of levitation, as the politicians and economists struggle to conjure new explanations, it starts to dawn on us that behind the curtain, at the heart of the Emerald City, sits not the benign and omnipotent invisible hand we had been promised, but something else entirely. Something responsible for what Marx, writing not so long before Conrad, cast as the 'everlasting uncertainty and anguish' of the 'bourgeois epoch'; a time in which 'all that is solid melts into air, all that is holy is profaned'. Draw back the curtain, follow the tireless motion of cogs and wheels back to its source, and you will find the engine driving our civilisation: the myth of progress.

The myth of progress is to us what the myth of god-given warrior prowess was to the Romans, or the myth of eternal salvation was to the conquistadors: without it, our efforts cannot be sustained. Onto the root stock of Western Christianity, the Enlightenment at its most optimistic grafted a vision of an Earthly paradise, towards which human effort guided by calculative reason could take us. Following this guidance, each generation will live a better life than the life of those that went before it. History becomes an escalator, and the only way is up. On the top floor is human perfection. It is important that this should remain just out of reach in order to sustain the sensation of motion.

Recent history, however, has given this mechanism something of a battering. The past century too often threatened a descent into hell, rather than the promised heaven on Earth. Even within the prosperous and liberal societies of the West progress has, in many ways, failed to deliver the goods. Today's generation is demonstrably less content, and consequently less optimistic, than those that went before. They work longer hours, with less security, and less chance of leaving behind the social background into which they were born. They fear crime, social breakdown, overdevelopment, environmental collapse. They do not believe that the future will be better than the past. Individually, they are less constrained by class and convention than their parents or grandparents, but more constrained by law, surveillance, state proscription and personal debt. Their physical health is better, their mental health more fragile. Nobody knows what is coming. Nobody wants to look.

Most significantly of all, there is an underlying darkness at the root of everything we have built. Outside the cities, beyond the blurring edges of our civilisation, at the mercy of the machine but not under its control, lies something that neither Marx nor Conrad, Caesar nor Hume, Thatcher nor Lenin ever really understood. Something that Western civilisation – which has set the terms for global civilisation –

was never capable of understanding, because to understand it would be to undermine, fatally, the myth of that civilisation. Something upon which that thin crust of lava is balanced; which feeds the machine and all the people who run it, and which they have all trained themselves not to see.

II: THE SEVERED HAND

Then what is the answer? Not to be deluded by dreams.
To know that great civilisations have broken down into violence,
and their tyrants come, many times before.
When open violence appears, to avoid it with honor or choose
the least ugly faction; these evils are essential.
To keep one's own integrity, be merciful and uncorrupted
and not wish for evil; and not be duped
By dreams of universal justice or happiness. These dreams will
not be fulfilled.
To know this, and know that however ugly the parts appear
the whole remains beautiful. A severed hand
Is an ugly thing and man disseevered from the earth and stars
and his history . . . for contemplation or in fact . . .
Often appears atrociously ugly. Integrity is wholeness,
the greatest beauty is
Organic wholeness, the wholeness of life and things, the divine beauty
of the universe. Love that, not man

Apart from that, or else you will share man's pitiful
   confusions,
or drown in despair when his days darken.
   Robinson Jeffers, 'The Answer'

The myth of progress is founded on the myth of nature. The
first tells us that we are destined for greatness; the second
tells us that greatness is cost-free. Each is intimately bound
up with the other. Both tell us that we are apart from the
world; that we began grunting in the primeval swamps, as
a humble part of something called 'nature', which we have
now triumphantly subdued. The very fact that we have a
word for 'nature' is evidence that we do not regard ourselves as part of it. Indeed, our separation from it is a myth
integral to the triumph of our civilisation. We are, we tell
ourselves, the only species ever to have attacked nature and
won. In this, our unique glory is contained.

Outside the citadels of self-congratulation, lone voices
have cried out against this infantile version of the human
story for centuries, but it is only in the last few decades that
its inaccuracy has become laughably apparent. We are the
first generations to grow up surrounded by evidence that
our attempt to separate ourselves from 'nature' has been a
grim failure, proof not of our genius but our hubris. The attempt to sever the hand from the body has endangered the
'progress' we hold so dear, and it has endangered much of
'nature' too. The resulting upheaval underlies the crisis we
now face.

We imagined ourselves isolated from the source of our existence. The fallout from this imaginative error is all around
us: a quarter of the world's mammals are threatened with

imminent extinction; an acre and a half of rainforest is felled every second; 75 per cent of the world's fish stocks are on the verge of collapse; humanity consumes 25 per cent more of the world's natural 'products' than the Earth can replace – a figure predicted to rise to 80 per cent by mid-century. Even through the deadening lens of statistics, we can glimpse the violence to which our myths have driven us.

And over it all looms runaway climate change. Climate change, which threatens to render all human projects irrelevant; which presents us with detailed evidence of our lack of understanding of the world we inhabit while, at the same time, demonstrating that we are still entirely reliant upon it. Climate change, which highlights in painful colour the head-on crash between civilisation and 'nature'; which makes plain, more effectively than any carefully constructed argument or optimistically defiant protest, how the machine's need for permanent growth will require us to destroy ourselves in its name. Climate change, which brings home at last our ultimate powerlessness.

These are the facts, or some of them. Yet facts never tell the whole story. ('Facts,' Conrad wrote, in *Lord Jim*, 'as if facts could prove anything.') The facts of environmental crisis we hear so much about often conceal as much as they expose. We hear daily about the impacts of our activities on 'the environment' (like 'nature', this is an expression which distances us from the reality of our situation). Daily we hear, too, of the many 'solutions' to these problems: solutions which usually involve the necessity of urgent political agreement and a judicious application of human technological genius. Things may be changing, runs the narrative, but there is nothing we cannot deal with here, folks. We perhaps need to move faster, more urgently. Certainly we need to accelerate the pace of research and development. We accept that we must become more 'sustainable'. But everything will be fine. There will still be growth, there will still be progress: these things will continue, because they have to continue, so they cannot do anything but continue. There is nothing to see here. Everything will be fine.

We do not believe that everything will be fine. We are not even sure, based on current definitions of progress and improvement, that we want it to be. Of all humanity's delusions of difference, of its separation from and superiority to the living world which surrounds it, one distinction holds up better than most: we may well be the first species capable of effectively eliminating life on Earth. This is a hypothesis we seem intent on putting to the test. We are already responsible for denuding the world of much of its richness, magnificence, beauty, colour and magic, and we show no sign of slowing down. For a very long time, we imagined that 'nature' was something that happened elsewhere. The damage we did to it might be regrettable, but needed to be weighed against the benefits here and now. And in the worst case scenario, there would always be some kind of Plan B. Perhaps we would make for the moon, where we could survive in lunar colonies under giant bubbles as we planned our expansion across the galaxy.

But there is no Plan B and the bubble, it turns out, is where we have been living all the while. The bubble is that delusion of isolation under which we have laboured for so long. The bubble has cut us off from life on the only planet we have, or are ever likely to have. The bubble is civilisation.

Consider the structures on which that bubble has been built. Its foundations are geological: coal, oil, gas – millions upon millions of years of ancient sunlight, dragged from the depths of the planet and burned with abandon. On this base, the structure stands. Move upwards, and you pass through a jumble of supporting horrors: battery chicken sheds; industrial abattoirs; burning forests; beam-trawled ocean floors; dynamited reefs; hollowed-out mountains; wasted soil. Finally, on top of all these unseen layers, you reach the well-tended surface where you and I stand: unaware, or uninterested, in what goes on beneath us; demanding that the authorities keep us in the manner to which we have been accustomed; occasionally feeling twinges of guilt that lead us to buy organic chickens or locally produced lettuces; yet for the most part glutted, but not sated, on the fruits of the horrors on which our lifestyles depend.

We are the first generations born into a new and unprecedented age – the age of ecocide. To name it thus is not to presume the outcome, but simply to describe a process which is under way. The ground, the sea, the air, the elemental backdrops to our existence – all these our economics has taken for granted, to be used as a bottomless tip, endlessly able to dilute and disperse the tailings of our extraction, production, consumption. The sheer scale of the sky or the weight of a swollen river makes it hard to imagine that creatures as flimsy as you and I could do that much damage. Philip Larkin gave voice to this attitude, and the creeping, worrying end of it in his poem 'Going, Going':

> *Things are tougher than we are, just*
> *As earth will always respond*

However we mess it about;
Chuck filth in the sea, if you must:
The tides will be clean beyond.
– But what do I feel now? Doubt?

Nearly forty years on from Larkin's words, doubt is what all of us seem to feel, all of the time. Too much filth has been chucked in the sea and into the soil and into the atmosphere to make any other feeling sensible. The doubt, and the facts, have paved the way for a worldwide movement of environmental politics, which aimed, at least in its early, raw form, to challenge the myths of development and progress head on. But time has not been kind to the greens. Today's environmentalists are more likely to be found at corporate conferences hymning the virtues of 'sustainability' and 'ethical consumption' than doing anything as naive as questioning the intrinsic values of civilisation. Capitalism has absorbed the greens, as it absorbs so many challenges to its ascendancy. A radical challenge to the human machine has been transformed into yet another opportunity for shopping.

'Denial' is a hot word, heavy with connotations. When it is used to brand the remaining rump of climate change sceptics, they object noisily to the association with those who would rewrite the history of the Holocaust. Yet the focus on this dwindling group may serve as a distraction from a far larger form of denial, in its psychoanalytic sense. Freud wrote of the inability of people to hear things which did not fit with the way they saw themselves and the world. We put ourselves through all kinds of inner contortions, rather than look plainly at those things which challenge our fundamental understanding of the world.

Today, humanity is up to its neck in denial about what it has built, what it has become – and what it is in for. Ecological and economic collapse unfold before us and, if we acknowledge them at all, we act as if this were a temporary problem, a technical glitch. Centuries of hubris block our ears like wax plugs; we cannot hear the message which reality is screaming at us. For all our doubts and discontents, we are still wired to an idea of history in which the future will be an upgraded version of the present. The assumption remains that things must continue in their current direction: the sense of crisis only smudges the meaning of that 'must'. No longer a natural inevitability, it becomes an urgent necessity: we must find a way to go on having supermarkets and superhighways. We cannot contemplate the alternative.

And so we find ourselves, all of us together, poised trembling on the edge of a change so massive that we have no way of gauging it. None of us knows where to look, but all of us know not to look down. Secretly, we all think we are doomed: even the politicians think this; even the environmentalists. Some of us deal with it by going shopping. Some deal with it by hoping it is true. Some give up in despair. Some work frantically to try and fend off the coming storm.

Our question is: what would happen if we looked down? Would it be as bad as we imagine? What might we see? Could it even be good for us?

We believe it is time to look down.

III: UNCIVILISATION

Without mystery, without curiosity and without the form imposed by a partial answer, there can be no stories – only confessions, communiqués, memories and fragments of autobiographical fantasy which for the moment pass as novels.

John Berger, 'A Story for Aesop', from Keeping a Rendezvous

If we are indeed teetering on the edge of a massive change in how we live, in how human society itself is constructed, and in how we relate to the rest of the world, then we were led to this point by the stories we have told ourselves – above all, by the story of civilisation.

This story has many variants, religious and secular, scientific, economic and mystic. But all tell of humanity's original transcendence of its animal beginnings, our growing mastery over a 'nature' to which we no longer belong, and the glorious future of plenty and prosperity which will follow when this mastery is complete. It is the story of human centrality, of a species destined to be lord of all it surveys, unconfined by the limits that apply to other, lesser creatures.

What makes this story so dangerous is that, for the most part, we have forgotten that it is a story. It has been told so many times by those who see themselves as rationalists, even scientists; heirs to the Enlightenment's legacy – a legacy which includes the denial of the role of stories in making the world.

Humans have always lived by stories, and those with skill in telling them have been treated with respect and, often, a certain wariness. Beyond the limits of reason, reality remains mysterious, as incapable of being approached directly as a hunter's quarry. With stories, with art, with symbols and layers of meaning, we stalk those elusive aspects of reality that go undreamed of in our philosophy. The story-teller weaves the mysterious into the fabric of life, lacing it with the comic, the tragic, the obscene, making safe paths through dangerous territory.

Yet as the myth of civilisation deepened its grip on our thinking, borrowing the guise of science and reason, we began to deny the role of stories, to dismiss their power as something primitive, childish, outgrown. The old tales by which generations had made sense of life's subtleties and strangenesses were bowdlerised and packed off to the nursery. Religion, that bag of myths and mysteries, birthplace of the theatre, was straightened out into a framework of universal laws and moral account-keeping. The dream visions of the Middle Ages became the nonsense stories of Victorian childhood. In the age of the novel, stories were no longer the way to approach the deep truths of the world, so much as a way to pass time on a train journey. It is hard, today, to imagine that the word of a poet was once feared by a king.

Yet for all this, our world is still shaped by stories. Through television, film, novels and video games, we may be more thoroughly bombarded with narrative material than any people that ever lived. What is peculiar, however, is the carelessness with which these stories are channelled at us – as entertainment, a distraction from daily life, something to hold our attention to the other side of the ad break. There is little sense that these things make up the equipment by which we navigate reality. On the other hand, there are the serious stories told by economists, politicians, geneticists and corporate leaders. These are not presented as stories at all, but as direct accounts of how the world is. Choose between competing versions, then fight with those who chose differently. The ensuing conflicts play out on early-morning radio, in afternoon debates and late-night television pundit wars. And yet, for all the noise, what is striking is how much the opposing sides agree on: all their stories are only variants of the larger story of human centrality, of our ever-expanding control over 'nature', our right to perpetual economic growth, our ability to transcend all limits.

So we find ourselves, our ways of telling unbalanced, trapped inside a runaway narrative, headed for the worst kind of encounter with reality. In such a moment, writers, artists, poets and storytellers of all kinds have a critical role to play. Creativity remains the most uncontrollable of human forces: without it, the project of civilisation is inconceivable, yet no part of life remains so untamed and undomesticated. Words and images can change minds, hearts, even the course of history. Their makers shape the stories people carry through their lives, unearth old ones and breathe them back to life, add new twists, point to unexpected endings. It is time to pick up the threads and make the stories new, as they must always be made new, starting from where we are.

Mainstream art in the West has long been about shock; about busting taboos, about Getting Noticed. This has gone on for so long that it has become common to assert that in these ironic, exhausted, post-everything times, there are no taboos left to bust.

But there is one.

The last taboo is the myth of civilisation. It is built upon the stories we have constructed about our genius, our indestructibility, our manifest destiny as a chosen species. It is where our vision and our self-belief intertwine with our reckless refusal to face the reality of our position on this Earth. It has led the human race to achieve what it has achieved; and has led the planet into the age of ecocide. The two are intimately linked. We believe they must be decoupled if anything is to remain.

We believe that artists – which is to us the most welcoming of words, taking under its wing writers of all kinds, painters, musicians, sculptors, poets, designers, creators, makers of things, dreamers of dreams – have a responsibility to begin the process of decoupling. We believe that, in the age of ecocide, the last taboo must be broken – and that only artists can do it.

Ecocide demands a response. That response is too important to be left to politicians, economists, conceptual thinkers, number crunchers; too all-pervasive to be left to activists or campaigners. Artists are needed. So far, though, the artistic response has been muted. In between traditional nature poetry and agitprop, what is there? Where are the poems that have adjusted their scope to the scale of this challenge? Where are the novels that probe beyond the country house or the city centre? What new form of writing has emerged to challenge civilisation itself? What gallery mounts an exhibition equal to this challenge? Which musician has discovered the secret chord?

If the answers to these questions have been scarce up to now, it is perhaps both because the depth of collective denial is so great, and because the challenge is so very daunting. We are daunted by it, ourselves. But we believe it needs to be risen to. We believe that art must look over the edge, face the world that is coming with a steady eye, and rise to the challenge of ecocide with a challenge of its own: an artistic response to the crumbling of the empires of the mind.

This response we call Uncivilised art, and we are interested in one branch of it in particular: Uncivilised writing. Uncivilised writing is writing which attempts to stand outside the human bubble and see us as we are: highly evolved apes with an array of talents and abilities which we are unleashing without sufficient thought, control, compassion or intelligence. Apes who have constructed a sophisticated myth of their own importance with which to sustain their civilising project. Apes whose project has been to tame, to control, to subdue or to destroy – to civilise the forests, the deserts, the wild lands and the seas, to impose bonds on the minds of their own in order that they might feel nothing when they exploit or destroy their fellow creatures.

Against the civilising project, which has become the progenitor of ecocide, Uncivilised writing offers not a non-human perspective – we remain human and, even now, are not quite ashamed – but a perspective which sees us as one strand of a web rather than as the first palanquin in a glorious procession. It offers an unblinking look at the forces among which we find ourselves.

It sets out to paint a picture of homo sapiens which a being from another world or, better, a being from our own – a blue whale, an albatross, a mountain hare – might recognise as something approaching a truth. It sets out to tug our attention away from ourselves and turn it outwards; to uncentre our minds. It is writing, in short, which puts civilisation – and us – into perspective. Writing that comes not, as most writing still does, from the self-absorbed and self-congratulatory metropolitan centres of civilisation but from somewhere on its wilder fringes. Somewhere woody and weedy and largely avoided, from where insistent, uncomfortable truths about ourselves drift in; truths which we're not keen on hearing. Writing which unflinchingly stares us down, however uncomfortable this may prove.

It might perhaps be just as useful to explain what Uncivilised writing is not. It is not environmental writing, for there is much of that about already, and most of it fails to jump the barrier which marks the limit of our collective human ego; much of it, indeed, ends up shoring up that ego, and helping us to persist in our civilisational delusions. It is not nature writing, for there is no such thing as nature as distinct from people, and to suggest otherwise is to perpetuate the attitude which has brought us here. And it is not political writing, with which the world is already flooded, for politics is a human confection, complicit in ecocide and decaying from within.

Uncivilised writing is more rooted than any of these. Above all, it is determined to shift our worldview, not to feed into it. It is writing for outsiders. If you want to be loved, it might be best not to get involved, for the world, at least for a time, will resolutely refuse to listen.

A salutary example of this last point can be found in the fate of one of the twentieth century's most significant yet most neglected poets. Robinson Jeffers was writing Uncivilised verse seventy years before this manifesto was thought of, though he did not call it that. In his early poetic career, Jeffers was a star: he appeared on the cover of *Time* magazine, read his poems in the US Library of Congress and was respected for the alternative he offered to the Modernist juggernaut. Today his work is left out of anthologies, his name is barely known and his politics are regarded with suspicion. Read Jeffers's later work and you will see why.

His crime was to deliberately puncture humanity's sense of self-importance. His punishment was to be sent into a lonely literary exile from which, forty years after his death, he has still not been allowed to return.

But Jeffers knew what he was in for. He knew that nobody, in an age of 'consumer choice', wanted to be told by this stone-faced prophet of the California cliffs that 'it is good for man ... [t]o know that his needs and nature are no more changed in fact in ten thousand years than the beaks of eagles'. He knew that no comfortable liberal wanted to hear his angry warning, issued at the height of the Second World War:

> *Keep clear of the dupes that talk democracy*
> *And the dogs that talk revolution*
> *Drunk with talk, liars and believers ...*
> *Long live freedom, and damn the ideologies.*

His vision of a world in which humanity was doomed to destroy its surroundings and eventually itself ('I would burn my right hand in a slow fire / To change the future ... I should do foolishly') was furiously rejected in the rising age of consumer democracy which he also predicted ('Be happy, adjust your economics to the new abundance ...').

Jeffers, as his poetry developed, developed a philosophy too. He called it 'inhumanism'. It was, he wrote:

a shifting of emphasis and significance from man to notman; the rejection of human solipsism and recognition of the transhuman magnificence ... This manner of thought and feeling is neither misanthropic nor pessimist . . . It offers a reasonable detachment as rule of conduct, instead of love, hate and envy . . . it provides magnificence for the religious instinct, and satisfies our need to admire greatness and rejoice in beauty.

The shifting of emphasis from man to notman: this is the aim of Uncivilised writing. To 'unhumanize our views a little, and become confident / As the rock and ocean that we were made from'. This is not a rejection of our humanity – it is an affirmation of the wonder of what it means to be truly human. It is to accept the world for what it is and to make our home here, rather than dreaming of relocating to the stars, or existing in a Man-forged bubble and pretending to ourselves that there is nothing outside it to which we have any connection at all.

This, then, is the literary challenge of our age. So far, few have taken it up. The signs of the times flash out in urgent neon, but our literary lions have better things to read. Their art remains stuck in its own civilised bubble. The idea of civilisation is entangled, right down to its semantic roots, with city-dwelling, and this provokes a thought: if our writers seem unable to find new stories which might lead us through the times ahead, is this not a function of their metropolitan mentality? The big names of contemporary literature are equally at home in the fashionable quarters of London or New York, and their writing reflects the prejudices of the placeless, transnational elite to which they belong.

The converse also applies. Those voices which tell other stories tend to be rooted in a sense of place. Think of John Berger's novels and essays from the Haute-Savoie, or the depths explored by Alan Garner within a day's walk of his birthplace in Cheshire. Think of Wendell Berry or W. S. Merwin, Mary Oliver or Cormac McCarthy. Those whose writings approach the shores of the Uncivilised are those who know their place, in the physical sense, and who remain wary of the siren cries of metrovincial fashion and civilised excitement.

If we name particular writers whose work embodies what we are arguing for, the aim is not to place them more prominently on the existing map of literary reputations. Rather, as Geoff Dyer has said of Berger, to take their work seriously is to redraw the maps altogether – not only the map of literary reputations, but those by which we navigate all areas of life.

Even here, we go carefully, for cartography itself is not a neutral activity. The drawing of maps is full of colonial echoes. The civilised eye seeks to view the world from above, as something we can stand over and survey. The Uncivilised writer knows the world is, rather, something we are enmeshed in – a patchwork and a framework of places, experiences, sights, smells, sounds. Maps can lead, but can also mislead. Our maps must be the kind sketched in the dust with a stick, washed away by the next rain. They can be read only by those who ask to see them, and they cannot be bought.

This, then, is Uncivilised writing. Human, inhuman, stoic and entirely natural. Humble, questioning, suspicious of the big idea and the easy answer. Walking the boundaries and reopening old conversations. Apart but engaged, its practitioners always willing to get their hands dirty; aware, in fact, that dirt is essential; that keyboards should be tapped by those with soil under their fingernails and wilderness in their heads.

We tried ruling the world; we tried acting as God's steward, then we tried ushering in the human revolution, the age of reason and isolation. We failed in all of it, and our failure destroyed more than we were even aware of. The time for civilisation is past. Uncivilisation, which knows its flaws because it has participated in them; which sees unflinchingly and bites down hard as it records – this is the project we must embark on now. This is the challenge for writing – for art – to meet. This is what we are here for.

IV: TO THE FOOTHILLS!

One impulse from a vernal wood
May teach you more of man,
Of moral evil and of good,
Than all the sages can.
    William Wordsworth, 'The Tables Turned'

A movement needs a beginning. An expedition needs a base camp. A project needs a headquarters. Uncivilisation is our project, and the promotion of Uncivilised writing – and art – needs a base. We present this manifesto not simply because we have something to say – who doesn't? – but because we have something to do. We hope this manifesto has created a spark. If so, we have a responsibility to fan the flames. This is what we intend to do. But we can't do it alone.

This is a moment to ask deep questions and to ask them urgently. All around us, shifts are under way which suggest that our whole way of living is already passing into history. It is time to look for new paths and new stories, ones that can lead us through the end of the world as we know it and out the other side. We suspect that by questioning the foundations of civilisation, the myth of human centrality, our imagined isolation, we may find the beginning of such paths.

If we are right, it will be necessary to go literally Beyond the Pale. Outside the stockades we have built – the city walls, the original marker in stone or wood that first separated 'man' from 'nature'. Beyond the gates, out into the wilderness, is where we are headed. And there we shall make for the higher ground for, as Jeffers wrote, 'when the cities lie at the monster's feet / There are left the mountains'. We shall make the pilgrimage to the poet's Dark Mountain, to the great, immovable, inhuman heights which were here before us and will be here after, and from their slopes we shall look back upon the pinprick lights of the distant cities and gain perspective on who we are and what we have become.

This is the Dark Mountain project. It starts here.

Where will it end? Nobody knows. Where will it lead? We are not sure. Its first incarnation, launched alongside this manifesto, is a website, which points the way to the ranges. It will contain thoughts, scribblings, jottings, ideas; it will work up the project of Uncivilisation, and invite all comers to join the discussion.

Then it will become a physical object, because virtual reality is, ultimately, no reality at all. It will become a journal, of paper, card, paint and print; of ideas, thoughts, observations, mumblings; new stories, which will help to define the project – the school, the movement – of Uncivilised writing. It will collect the words and the images of those who consider themselves Uncivilised and have something to say about it; who want to help us attack the citadels. It will be a thing of beauty for the eye and for the heart and for the mind, for we are unfashionable enough to believe that beauty – like truth – not only exists, but still matters.

Beyond that . . . all is currently hidden from view. It is a long way across the plains, and things become obscured by distance. There are great white spaces on this map still. The civilised would fill them in; we are not so sure we want to. But we cannot resist exploring them, navigating by rumours and by the stars. We don't know quite what we will find. We are slightly nervous. But we will not turn back, for we believe that something enormous may be out there, waiting to meet us.

Uncivilisation, like civilisation, is not something that can be created alone. Climbing the Dark Mountain cannot be a solitary exercise. We need bearers, sherpas, guides, fellow adventurers. We need to rope ourselves together for safety. At present, our form is loose and nebulous. It will firm itself up as we climb. Like the best writing, we need to be shaped by the ground beneath our feet, and what we become will be shaped, at least in part, by what we find on our journey.

If you would like to climb at least some of the way with us, we would like to hear from you. We feel sure there are others out there who would relish joining us on this expedition.

Come. Join us. We leave at dawn.

The Eight Principles of Uncivilisation

We must unhumanize our views a little, and become confident
As the rock and ocean that we were made from.
Robinson Jeffers

1. We live in a time of social, economic and ecological unravelling. All around us are signs that our whole way of living is already passing into history. We will face this reality honestly and learn how to live with it.

2. We reject the faith that holds that the converging crises of our times can be reduced to a set of 'problems' in need of technological or political 'solutions'.

3. We believe that the roots of these crises lie in the stories we have been telling ourselves. We intend to challenge the stories that underpin our civilisation: the myth of progress, the myth of human centrality, and the myth of our separation from 'nature'. These myths are more dangerous for the fact that we have forgotten they are myths.

4. We will reassert the role of storytelling as more than mere entertainment. It is through stories that we weave reality.

5. Humans are not the point and purpose of the planet. Our art will begin with the attempt to step outside the human bubble. By careful attention, we will re-engage with the non-human world.

6. We will celebrate writing and art that is grounded in a sense of place and of time. Our literature has been dominated for too long by those who inhabit the cosmopolitan citadels.

7. We will not lose ourselves in the elaboration of theories or ideologies. Our words will be elemental. We write with dirt under our fingernails.

8. The end of the world as we know it is not the end of the world full stop. Together, we shall find the hope beyond hope, the paths that lead to the unknown world ahead of us.

2009

PAUL KINGSNORTH is the author of *Alexandria*, *Beast*, and *The Wake*, which won the 2014 Gordon Burn Prize, was longlisted for the Man Booker Prize, the Folio Prize, and the Desmond Elliott Prize, and was shortlisted for the Goldsmith's Prize. He is co-founder of the Dark Mountain Project, a global network of writers, artists, and thinkers in search of new stories for a world on the brink.

Confessions of a Recovering Environmentalist and Other Essays was typeset by Faber and Faber Limited. Manufactured by Versa Press on acid-free, 30 percent postconsumer wastepaper.